THE IRONIC STATE

British Comedy and the Everyday
Politics of Globalization

James Brassett

BRISTOL
UNIVERSITY
PRESS

First published in Great Britain in 2021 by Bristol University Press

Bristol University Press
University of Bristol
1–9 Old Park Hill
Bristol
BS2 8BB
UK
t: +44 (0)117 954 5940
e: bup-info@bristol.ac.uk

Details of international sales and distribution partners are available at bristoluniversitypress.co.uk

British Library Cataloguing in Publication Data
A catalogue record for this book is available from the British Library

ISBN 978-1-5292-0845-0 hardcover
ISBN 978-1-5292-0848-1 ePub
ISBN 978-1-5292-0847-4 ePdf

Cover design: blu inc, Bristol
Front cover image: Eva Bee, Ikon Images
Bristol University Press uses environmentally responsible print partners.
Printed and bound in Great Britain by CPI Group (UK) Ltd, Croydon, CR0 4YY

Contents

Acknowledgements

Numerous people have encouraged and supported me along the path that led to this book. It took quite some time and several articles before I really believed this could be a research project, instead of a few neat examples of subversion in International Relations and International Political Economy. In that sense, I am indebted to several editors and anonymous reviewers who have pushed me, sometimes generously, sometimes hard, to take comedy more seriously. He is gone now, but Nick Rengger was there at the start and got me going. Erzsebet Strausz inspired me to go back to comedy and resistance at a crucial point. Alex Sutton has been generous with his vast knowledge of (and ability with) British comedy. Chris Rossdale has humoured me on questions of resistance even when my intent seemed frivolous. Chris Browning has helped me to see new ways forward on humour that I am excited to be turning to now. I am grateful to colleagues at the University of Warwick for sharing countless conversations and (occasionally intense) drinks. In particular, Richard Aldrich, Shaun Breslin, Andre Broome, Chris Clarke, Mat Clayton, Juanita Elias, Shirin Rai, Lena Rethel, Ben Richardson, Chris Rogers and Nick Vaughan-Williams. Beyond the bubble, I am grateful to Dan Bulley and Cian O'Driscoll for always reminding me of the importance of puns. Friendly encouragement from Roland Bleiker, Matt Davies, Kyle Grayson, Amanda Kallstig, Sharon Lockyer, Ben Rosamond, Robert Saunders, Len Seabrooke, Brent Steele, Simon Weaver and Alister Wedderburn was important at different points. I thank my editor Stephen Wenham and the whole team at Bristol University Press for making this such an enjoyable experience from start to finish. Comedy is important for all sorts of reasons, but the key one for me is to hear the laughter of my wife Olivia and our daughter Isabella.

Introduction: Comedy and the Politics of (Global) Resistance

British comedy is a widely consumed and distinctive cultural product. For some the British are virtually defined by their sense of irony, or a tendency for self-deprecation (Friedman, 2011; see also Fox, 2014). But humour and comedy are far more than static stereotypes. Over several decades, British comedy has emerged as a vibrant, productive, conflictual and *avowedly resistant* discourse within politics. From the 1960s 'satire boom' that chided the imperial pomposity of the upper-class establishment, through 1980s 'alternative comedy' that articulated dissent against Thatcher to embrace equality politics, and the rise of 'radical comedy' in the post-crisis, anti-austerity mode of Russell Brand or Charlie Brooker, British comedy has emerged as a vernacular through which resistance is imagined and performed (Brassett, 2016).

How can humour be resistant when it is part of a massive global industry? British comedy is big business. Sell-out tours, DVD sales, and cash-in memoirs are part of a burgeoning global entertainment industry. Keynote acts and producers like John Oliver, Ricky Gervais, Armando Iannucci and Richard Curtis straddle the lucrative US and UK markets. Comedy output by the BBC, Channel 4 and Sky is regularly distributed through global platforms like HBO, Netflix and Amazon. Yet British comedy is also a sophisticated genre that combines mainstream popularity with a capacity to challenge and provoke. Indeed, such provocation can be part of the schtick. As every satirist knows, controversy is good publicity and the moralizing think-piece industry has helped promote acts like Sacha Baron Cohen and Frankie Boyle (Hunt, 2010). The regular rehearsal of offence and outrage at jokes highlights a mismatch between the ideal of comic resistance and the material success *and celebrity status* of comedians (Lockyer and Pickering, 2009). Especially in a period of austerity, the radical politics of many comedians seems to fly in the face of their position within an immensely successful global industry.

Comedy thus animates broader dilemmas over the politics resistance. What do we resist and how? How do practices of resistance engage with – and sometimes reproduce – wider structures of power? To what extent is resistance recuperated within the cultural logic of global capitalism (Vintaghen and Johansson, 2013; Rossdale, 2019; see also Jameson, 1991)? In figuring comedy as a practice of *everyday resistance* in global context, this book develops a specific contribution to the study of comedy and politics. While existing research has questioned the *political impact* of British comedy, such work is marked out by an almost exclusively state-centric understanding of what politics is and where it happens, that is, in parliament, conducted by politicians (Brassett and Sutton, 2017). By situating British comedy in the context of imperial decline, liberalization, and an ongoing (if awkward) embrace of globalization, an everyday approach can yield important insights on the politics of comic resistance; how agency is constituted; and how global rationalities are accommodated (or not).

My central argument is that British comedy provides a culturally resonant and socially situated vernacular of everyday political engagement. A widely known 'weapon of the weak' (Scott, 1987), comedy, joking and satire have infused vast swathes of British culture, while ostensibly falling below the radar of 'Big History'. The way comedy and satire portray Britain's place in the world can be an important archive of global politics: How is imperial decline satirized? What possibilities and limits are constituted by 'alternative comedy'? Does 1990s irony mark a critique of or accommodation to globalization, as satires of political correctness integrate with commodity culture? With its various considerations of empire, the class system and capitalism, British comedy includes an insightful set of popular reflections on the politics of globalization: how markets are lived, legitimated and contested. In this way, as Chapter 1 will discuss, the book is also located within the *everyday turn* in International Relations (IR) and International Political Economy (IPE) that emphasizes the constitutive agency of (apparently) marginal actors and domains like popular culture in world politics (Hobson and Seabrooke, 2007; Grayson et al, 2009; Best and Paterson, 2010).

Throughout the book, however, British comedy will also be a subject of critique. As an everyday practice of resistance, comedy is *always-already* located in a complex set of global power relations. For example, despite the anti-establishment tones of the satire boom, many of its protagonists were white, male, Oxbridge graduates. Not only did they come to form a new media elite as they crossed over into TV and Hollywood but, as Chapter 2 will discuss, they were also party to the marginalization of alternative 'comic voices', from the exclusion of women in Footlights, to the use of racist stereotypes in *Beyond the Fringe* and *Monty Python* (Wilmut, 1980; Wagg, 1992). Recognizing such contingencies and ambiguities is normally an invitation to discount resistance, or suggest that it has failed in some way. However, I will argue that it can provoke important questions about what's at stake in the move to value resistance, helping us to elucidate the social and political struggles that go on *within* everyday global resistance. Thus, the historical excavation of a comic vernacular is also a precursor to an alternative politics of comedy, which can reflect – *inter alia* – the rise of feminist and postcolonial satires within/against the British comedy establishment and, more recently, the generalization of satirical literacy via social media and meme culture. Comic resistance as a site of politics, not an end.

Ultimately, the book provides a story about how global market life is lived, contested and accommodated. Against those who would like to 'utilize' comedy – or indeed resistance more broadly – as straightforward dissent that follows a logic of opposition *against* power, I seek to draw out the complex entwinement between comic resistances and the (re-)fashioning of power over time. Neither an escape from the hard questions of politics, nor a passive archive that simply reflects upon wider global change, British comedy yields a performative politics of globalization, whereby the resistant practices of comedy and satire both question *and enact* the political possibilities and limits of market life. Comedy is thus an everyday vernacular through which subjects emerge *as global, as political*.

This Introduction situates the approach of the book within existing debates on comedy and politics. Section 1 addresses two broad and popular frameworks, which I label 'Instrumental' and 'Critical'. They each provide good reasons to be sceptical of the role of comedy in politics by questioning the *actual impact* it can have. Section 2 outlines the approach of this book, to think about comedy as an everyday practice of global resistance. While sympathetic to existing frameworks, not least, because they underline the potential significance of comedy, I make the case for a performative approach (Butler, 1993, 2010). I argue that we should think about comedy and satire as ongoing practices of politics, not some artificially separate domain that may impact upon 'it'. This framework draws on different authors of comic resistance like Bakhtin (1984) and Orwell (1945), yet it places greater emphasis on the cultural context and performativity of jokes. In methodological terms, then, my focus is on the question: *what is left behind?* Too often, the politics of comedy is a one-off moment of 'impact': how a comedian or joke brings down a politician or their party. Instead, my research will focus on how the vernacular of British comedy *emerges* over time to provide a language, a set of techniques that can underpin a *productive politics* of resistance. Section 3 will then provide the outline for the book.

1 Comedy and politics: two approaches

How should we think about the relationship between comedy and politics? One way might be to use existing theories of comedy, which carry a long history spanning distinct traditions and disciplinary commitments (Morreal, 1987; Critchley, 2002). Broadly, there are three approaches, which all suggest important insights for thinking about the role of comedy in political resistance: 'superiority', 'incongruity' and 'relief'.

First, the 'superiority' theory of comedy understands joking as a potentially blunt assertion of social hierarchy, as when someone is 'the butt of the joke'. The superiority theory 'argues that humour and laughter are created from and convey a sense of superiority over the object of laughter. Humour is described as a means of mocking and ridiculing the subject of the joke, so describing laughter as invective' (Weaver, 2011: 14). It is not hard to see the political function of such jokes insofar as they can be mobilized to suppress and exclude marginal groups or apparent 'others', for example in terms of humour that is racist, sexist, xenophobic, ableist, etc. Second, the 'incongruity' theory suggests that a joke elicits laughter as a reaction to our 'perception of incongruous elements, such as the experience of the unexpected, or two objects being placed together in an unusual way' (Weaver, 2011: 18). In terms of politics, this can be read into arguments about the subversive potential of humour to reveal the way social and political hierarchies depend upon certain silences and fabrications to survive. And, third, the 'relief' theory of comedy suggests that jokes can *relieve* the tension in social situations, allowing for a moment of shared relaxation or even catharsis (Freud, 2003). On this view, humour can play the role of a 'safety valve' in difficult political circumstances, like crisis or war, for example, gallows humour or, at the subjective level, as a form of psychological displacement (Steele, forthcoming).

While these theories can be mobilized for understanding the workings of political humour, I would argue that they do not suffice to form the basis of an approach to comedy and politics, more broadly. At one level, I would argue that we need an approach that can take account of the fact that comedy does different things, in different contexts. Much of the theoretical work on humour has been focused on the 'success' of comedy, that is to say, what makes a joke work, that is, *what makes you laugh?* While an important consideration, not least for comedians themselves, it is of limited utility for thinking about the relationship between comedy and the wider realm of politics, with its power relations, hierarchies and contests. Here, we might be rather more concerned with the political context and the broader effects and implications of jokes; including, for instance, their circulation and reception, the politics of offence or, indeed, their various political economies of production and consumption. At another level, and building from this more complex appreciation, we should remain acutely aware of how comedy can serve different political functions. Broadly speaking, there seems to be both a *critical* and a *conservative* function in humour; that is to say, jokes can either politicize or de-politicize. For instance, some combination of 'relief' and 'incongruity' might create a form of ironic distance, which can aid political reflection in the context of uncertainty. However, another combination of 'relief' and 'superiority' could stifle such potentials, by simply affirming the prejudices of the in-group, that is, those who 'get the joke'. Indeed, this is a common ambiguity in the discourse of a national sense of humour (Brassett, 2009; Kuipers, 2011).

Drawing these points together, a political analysis of comedy therefore requires a facility for critical judgement that goes beyond evaluations of why a joke 'succeeds' or 'fails', in order to ask about its broader fit with a social and political context of hierarchy, identity and disagreement. Often the fact that a joke *does not work*, or is perceived to be 'unfunny', may be just as politically significant because it tells us something about the terms of political relation. As Lauren Berlant and Sianne Ngai (2017: 234–5) argue, this can be an uncomfortable process, which is *precisely why* it is political:

> Comedy's propensity to get in trouble – sometimes greater even than genres like horror or porn – gets thrown into sharper relief when we think of it as a vernacular form. What we find comedic (or just funny) is sensitive to changing contexts. It is sensitive because the funny is always tripping over the not funny, sometimes appearing identical

to it. [...] Comedy helps us test or figure out what it means to say 'us'. Always crossing lines, it helps us figure out what lines we desire or can bear.

The prevailing frameworks for thinking about comedy in political science and political philosophy do not so much concern themselves with how jokes work, as their *political significance*. What is the wider political function of comedy? How does humour or satire support wider concerns with progress, democratic deliberation, questions of resistance and change? While these research questions require some basic understanding of humour, they are rather more concerned with a critical orientation to the power political dimensions of comedy. For example, in a British context, we might therefore focus on the role of humour and joking in the reconstruction of racist social relations (Weaver, 2011), or else, the capacity of satirical work to 'punch up' against the various forms of privilege in the social order (Flinders, 2013). Simply put, *who gets to joke?* What relations of power and violence both permit and emerge from British comedy?

The instrumental approach

A first framework for thinking about comedy and politics focuses on the question of 'impact'. On this view, we should judge comedy on its capacity to serve a political purpose. For instance, comedy might enrich the critical potential of society, or engage citizens in the political life of the state. This tradition of thought can cite the example of political satire like Jonathan Swift's 'modest proposal', which satirized English colonial attitudes towards Ireland. It further draws on such luminaries as George Orwell to argue that the 'point' of comedy and satire is to trouble the powerful to the benefit of the afflicted. The instrumental approach therefore identifies with and builds from the idea that comedy and satire should 'punch up'. As George Orwell (1945) argued in a critique of *Punch* magazine:

> A thing is funny when ... it upsets the established order. Every joke is a tiny revolution. If you had to define humour in a single phrase, you might define it as dignity sitting on a tin-tack. Whatever destroys dignity, and brings down the mighty from their seats, preferably with a bump, is funny. And the bigger the fall, the bigger the joke. It would be better fun to throw a custard pie at a bishop than at a curate. With this general principle in mind, one can, I think, begin

to see what has been wrong with English comic writing during the present century.

This framework for thinking about comedy and politics is appealing because it speaks to a rationalist set of political commitments about citizenship, deliberation and a well-functioning civil society. Indeed, the instrumental approach to comedy also has a palpable lineage in the public discussion of comedy. It has featured in debates over whether the 'satire boom' sold out (Wagg, 2002); if alternative comedy was an effective challenge to Thatcher, or whether shows like *Spitting Image* just made her more popular (Schaffer, 2016); and, more recently, questions about the desirability of politicians appearing on panel shows like *Have I Got News For You* (Higgie, 2017). In turn, however, I would argue that the instrumental approach produces a somewhat truncated mode of judgement. That is to say, *either* comedy is beneficial to politics, or, *more commonly*, it is deeply flawed, even counter-productive to the values of participatory democratic politics. As Julie Webber (2013: 7) observes, 'few political science scholars examine political comedy, and when they do, they ask an outdated disciplinary question: does it promote civic engagement? Or does it make citizens cynical toward government?'

The instrumental approach can therefore result in a *lament* for a particular kind of politics. This has played out in a growing scepticism towards the role of humour and satire in British politics. Satirizing politicians and political parties is argued to foster cynicism and apathy among citizens (Fielding, 2014a, 2014b). In more sweeping variants, a norm of subversion and *snark* within the public sphere is associated with the 'hollowing out' of political life as reason and deliberation are replaced by personality politics and soundbite culture (Denby, 2010; Flinders, 2013). A kind of 'post-truth' malaise emerges whereby politicians themselves – most notably Boris Johnson – enjoy a symbiotic relationship with satire (Iannucci, 2015, 2016). Indeed, Jonathan Coe (2013) drew a typically biting line from Peter Cook to suggest that the rise of Boris Johnson, insulated by the cloak of irony and laughter, suggests that the UK political system is in danger of '*sinking giggling into the sea*'.

A key proposition of this approach is that British comedy and satire carries the potential for an excessive and personal critique of politicians, which fosters a negative view among the audience, that is, voters. In a comparative study, Van Zoonen and Wring (2012) found that US fiction and satire tended to be optimistic or inspiring in tone, while British political comedies were more likely to portray politicians as dim-witted or selfish, with a generally gloomy outlook. The political function of British comedy can therefore become conservative, foster apathy, and turn away from democratic values. As Steven Fielding (2011) argues, comedy 'has always relied on stereotypes. There was a time when the Irish were thick; the Scots were careful with money; mothers-in-law fierce and ugly; and the Welsh stole and shagged sheep. The corrupt politician is one such stereotype, one that is neither racist nor sexist and seemingly acceptable to all.'

On this view, the instrumental approach can provide a clear and critical perspective on the relationship between comedy and politics. For all the apparent critical potential of comedy and satire, the normalization of humour and joking about politicians has become prone to fostering apathy and disengagement. It merely provides a laugh followed by a stoic shrug of the shoulders. As Matt Flinders (2013) surmised: 'there has been a groundswell of opinion against political comedy and satire as evidence grows of its social impact and generally negative social influence (especially over the young)'. While this lament for younger people was targeted at the rise of Russell Brand, Flinders considered that there was more going on: 'in recent years the nature of political comedy and satire has derived great pleasure and huge profits from promoting corrosive cynicism rather than healthy scepticism'.

To underline, the instrumental approach is an enormously influential framework, one that is also a socially resonant discourse. As Chapters 2 and 7 will consider, the instrumental approach has figured in public debates about the satire boom, as well as Brexit and the 'failure' of comedy to check the rise of populism. Indeed, the instrumental approach even feeds into comedy itself, with Stewart Lee (2014a) channelling the critique to argue that Boris Johnson has become the world's first *self-satirizing* politician:

> Johnson's trademark tuck-shop wit makes him a formidable political orator. Johnson is like an iron fist encased in an iron glove, but on the knuckles of the iron glove are tiny childlike drawings of ejaculating penises at which even the son of a Marxist intellectual cannot help but smirk.

In different ways, therefore, and with a considerable degree of acceptance by wider publics, the instrumental approach can provide an important set of insights on the relationship between comedy and politics. Does comedy challenge the powerful or does it merely excuse them with a few laughs?

The critical approach

The second approach to comedy is related to the first, but orients to a more reflective set of questions about the political and philosophical basis of humour and joking. Writers in this tradition seek to unpick questions of how and why comedy is an important cultural practice that carries an implicit set of critical dimensions. While echoing the instrumental approach in terms of recognizing an implicit association between humour and resistance, the critical approach makes a number of propositions about the *complicity* (or not) between comedy and wider social structures of modernity, capitalism and individualism. In this sense, while they both plough a similar furrow, the instrumental approach is far more focused on the synchronic relations between comedy and politics, seeking to assess 'impact' in the here-and-now, while the critical approach draws upon a set of questions that run diachronically, situating the political function of comedy over time.

A critical approach to comedy and politics begins from the idea that humour and laughter can be a profoundly important practice within social and political life. While Orwell (1945) provides a nice rhetorical quip that every joke is like a 'tiny revolution', authors in the critical tradition are prone to expand such sentiments to imagine the utopian, radical and normative possibilities of comedy and laughter. Quintessentially, Mikhail Bakhtin (1984) identified a form of humour that resided in the folk practices of peasant communities, which could be mobilized in times of 'carnival' to manifest a socially inclusive moment of political resistance. For Bakhtin, laughter 'has a deep philosophical meaning, it is one of the essential forms of truth concerning the world as a whole, concerning history and man; it is a peculiar point of view relative to the world; the world is seen anew, no less (and perhaps more) profoundly than when seen from the serious standpoint' (Bakhtin, 1984: 66). Further, when laughter was mobilized through the 'the people' at times of carnival, Bakhtin envisaged a utopic potential; that the celebration of the body, especially the lower strata, could manifest a popular irreverence in the face of 'seriousness':

> The carnivalesque crowd in the marketplace or in the streets is not merely a crowd. It is the people as a whole, but organized in their own way, the way of the people. It is outside of and contrary to all existing forms of the coercive socioeconomic and political organization, which is suspended for the time of the festivity. (1984: 255)

On this view, the revolutionary potential of jokes is more than rhetoric and can be a popular practice of emancipation. In the critical approach, humour and laughter can provide a deep, potentially universal force of truth, against structures of power and seriousness that seem to repress and discipline. However, if these high ideals about laughter are an emancipatory possibility, then the critical approach is less optimistic about realizing them through modern comedy. In Bakhtin's own work, his celebration of the medieval carnivalesque was contrasted with the decline and neutering of European carnivals over time. Indeed, he actively contrasted the 'joyful, open, festive laugh' of the carnival with the 'closed, purely negative, satirical laugh' of modern comedy, which he argued was 'not a laughing laugh …' (Bakhtin, 1984: 134–5). This foregrounds a key problematic of comic resistance: is comedy ever 'truly resistant', or is it just a technique for tranquillizing dissent? As Slavoj Žižek (2008: 24) argues, 'in contemporary societies … cynical distance, laughter, irony, are, so to speak, part of the game. The ruling ideology is not meant to be taken seriously or literally.'

The critical approach can yield two important lines of reflection that are useful for thinking about British comedy. First, by foregrounding the emancipatory potential of laughter, it provokes us to think carefully about the actual relationship between humour and resistance. While the practices and form of comedy may seem intuitively resistant, laughing at, taking the piss, subverting, etc., the critical approach draws attention to the wider social and historical function of comedy. Is professional comedy complicit with the wider commodification of culture? Does it merely provide some light relief from the daily grind of capitalist alienation? On this view, instead of the emancipatory laughter of the people, we now observe 'consumers' in comedy clubs, or TV viewers who passively receive copyrighted 'content'. As Horkheimer and Adorno (1979: 140) suggest, such '[f]un is a medicinal bath. The pleasure industry never fails to prescribe it. It makes laughter the instrument of the fraud practised on happiness.' Second, building on the wider social function of humour, a number of authors have wondered about the sociological effects of jokes in modernity. If comedy and laughter yields an individualizing effect in late capitalism, providing a cheap laugh to cleanse the alienated worker, then what about the nature of joking itself? In this vein, and drawing on the superiority theory of comedy, Bergson argued:

> society holds over each individual member, if not the threat of correction, at all events the prospect of a snubbing, which, although it is slight, is none the less dreaded. Such

> must be the function of laughter. Always rather humiliating
> for the one against whom it is directed, laughter is really
> and truly a kind of social ragging. (Bergson, 1911: 135)

On this view, the 'othering' potential of humour is not just an unfortunate side effect of a poorly conceived joke, but rather an essential element in the everyday violence of comedy. In his book *Laughter and Ridicule*, Michael Billig (2005) argues that ridicule is not some accidental element in comedy, but is actually a central component of its sociological function. Ridicule ensures that people comply with established customs and habits. Far from the critical ideal of 'pure resistance' then, this 'imparts to humour a key role in social discipline and the maintenance of social order' (Lockyer and Pickering, 2008: 814). Across these different concerns with the social and political function of humour and comedy, the critical approach raises some important and influential questions for thinking about comedy and politics. Is comedy truly resistant? What role can humour and laughter play in resistance, after the commodification of comedy? How should we think about the disciplinary potential of laughter and ridicule in modern societies?

2 The approach of this book

While sympathetic to the existing theoretical work on comedy and politics, this book will develop an approach that differs in some important respects. With reference to the 'instrumental approach', I argue that there is a problematic state-centrism in the analysis, which can downplay the global context of British comedy while figuring 'politics' itself in a circumscribed way, that is, as something conducted by politicians in parliament. At one level, it risks overlooking the multiple ways in which the history of British comedy has been inflected by (and become resistant to) global political concerns – *inter alia* imperial decline, de-industrialization, immigration, neoliberalism, austerity, etc. Thus, it is not simply a question of how comedy and satire speak to one or other side of the parliamentary divide, but how they embody and enact the everyday politics of globalization. At another level, in presenting such a limited view of the relationship between comedy and politics this approach reduces potential judgements to a rationalist diagnosis of 'impact'. Broadly speaking, I question the objective separation between a domain of 'culture' on the one hand, and a domain of 'politics', on the other. While this may be a handy reflex to check the rise (and profits) of comedians and the comedy business, it is sociologically anaemic when set against the disciplinary effects of comedy identified by the critical approach. On this view, comedy is not 'good' or 'bad' for politics. Comedy *is* politics (Brassett and Sutton, 2017).

However, while my approach is animated by themes and dilemmas identified by the critical approach, I am equally cautious of reifying a vision of resistance as being an 'all-or-nothing' question. On this view, the critical approach can sometimes over determine what resistance is, or what it should do. *Either* resistance is figured as a 'pure', universal form of truth, emancipation – as per Bakhtin's foundation, the 'utopian laughter' of 'the people' – *or* humour and comedy are condemned to play the role of ideological smokescreen: the 'cheap' laughs of the 'culture industry', which provide the ameliorative giggle so workers can ignore their alienation (Sutton, forthcoming). While these are important critical reflexes, they carry a potentially totalizing view of resistance. On this view, resistance is either 'pure' (read: emancipatory), or it is merely 'recuperated' within the social power relations it is supposed to contest. Instead, this book will develop a more *productive* image of resistance; one that remains open to how comic resistances are able to perform new rationalities and subjectivities over time.

In essence, the book is guided by an ontology of resistance as creative, prefigurative even (Rossdale, 2019). Everyday resistance *produces* things. Too often resistance is figured as some kind of opposite to power, a physical force that works against an apparently prior set of power relations. This delineation of objective oppositions arguably underpins some of the rationalist dilemmas of 'impact' and 'purity' identified in the previous section. Indeed, when we think about resistance in politics, we often associate it with a particular agent, such as trade unions, civil society, or in this case, the comedian. So the logic goes, when resistance does not live up to our prior theoretical expectations, then obviously, it must be because one or other agent has been recuperated, co-opted or 'sold out': Ben Elton, for example. Instead, what would it mean to think of resistance as a *productive* element *within* power relations? As Foucault (1990: 95–6) argued, this would begin the process of de-linking practices of resistance from wider theories of it:

> there is no single locus of great Refusal, no soul of revolt, source of all rebellions, or pure law of the revolutionary. Instead there is a plurality of resistances, each of them a special case [...] by definition they can only exist in the strategic field of power relations. But this does not mean that they are only a reaction or a rebound, forming with

respect to the basic domination an underside that is in the end always passive, doomed to perpetual defeat. Resistances do not derive from a few heterogenous principles; but neither are they a lure or a promise that is of necessity betrayed. They are the odd term in relations of power; they are inscribed in the latter as an irreducible opposite.

On this view, comedy is not required to live up to some predefined ideal of 'impacting' on the election, or realizing the 'real' interests of the people. Instead, comedy and joking can be understood as a productive element within the social power relations of everyday life. By developing the importance of everyday acts of resistance (Scott, 1987) in combination with a more productive understanding of power relations, Chapter 1 will re-describe British comedy as an everyday practice of resistance in global context.

Drawing these points together, my central argument re-describes humour and comedy as a contingent and emergent vernacular of politics. The craft of British comedy, including its professional norms and structures, the language of satire and the subversion it fosters, and the way jokes circulate in the public sphere, all combine to manifest a productive language of engagement. To qualify, it may not bring down a leader, or overturn the class system, but it performs important new rationalities and subjectivities (Brassett, 2016). In a word, the vernacular of comic resistance circulates and changes over time. The competitive nature of British comedy can produce rivalries and hostilities among comedians themselves, as each new generation seeks to outdo the previous one. But even this 'marketized' concentration around professional esteem (and rivalry) creates a peculiar obsession with 'the Canon' that carries a productive possibility. Crucially, the chapters that follow detail how many of these rivalries manifest over *the question of resistance itself*, whereby, for example, the previously lauded heroes of the satire boom were castigated by alternative comedians for their class and gender privilege. In this sense, the everyday vernacular of comic resistance is in a constant state of emergence and development – a kind of reflexive public sphere – at its best, seeking to understand and subvert its own position within global power relations (Brassett, 2009).

The specific contribution of this approach to the study of comedy and politics is twofold. First, it situates the study of British comedy in a global context of imperial decline, deregulation, neoliberalism and globalization. My approach to British comedy, understood as an everyday practice of resistance, reflects the emergence of new rationalities and subjectivities of global politics. This includes a critical engagement with the possibilities and limits of, for instance, the satirical news format, the association of comedy with egalitarianism, irony over political correctness, the subversion of postcolonial charity campaigns, and the rise of 'citizen satire' through meme culture. Second, it draws out the commonalities, debates and divergences that operate *within* the everyday vernacular of British comedy to identify how it is a rich and resonant tradition of popular culture in world politics. In this sense, the significance of comic resistance is not limited to a universalist philosophical interest in 'purity' or 'emancipation', but is rather figured as part of the popular cultural politics through which global change is contested, rejected, accommodated and legitimated. Neither a panacea for the hard questions of political resistance, nor a simple strategic agent for political 'impact', British comedy is an everyday vernacular of political engagement that can provide insightful reflections on the changing context and everyday agency for practising global resistance.

3 Outline

The book will proceed in seven chapters. The first chapter will situate the study of British comedy in the theoretical and methodological literature on the everyday turn in global politics. The burgeoning field of everyday politics suggests a number of links between everyday resistance and the politics of globalization. Although the everyday literature has done much to decentre IR and IPE from their methodological dichotomies of international–domestic, high–low politics and so on, I argue that we need to pay more attention to the ambiguities and emergent potentialities of everyday resistance. It is in the contests, negotiations and accommodations that go on within everyday practices of resistance that the politics of globalization is located. Having established the framework of everyday global resistance, the following chapters will turn to the (global) history of British comedy. The second chapter will address the satire boom as a cultural economy of decline. Central themes include the satirization of arrogance and pomposity associated with the imperial elite, as well as, a profound sense of doubt and self-deprecation over Britain's new-found lack of a role in global politics. The third chapter deals with a more mature version of British comedy in the rise of alternative comedy. Here comedy takes on an avowed sense of political identity, questioning social attitudes and orienting against neoliberalism. A fourth chapter deals with the rise of irony and questions an essential ambiguity that emerges in comedy of this period. On the one hand, new satires by Chris Morris and Armando Iannucci advance a set of post-structural concerns with the mediatization of politics and the loss of a coherent subject. On the other hand, the apparent return of reactionary subjects of race, gender and sexuality in the work of Sacha Baron Cohen and Ricky Gervais suggests that irony plays an important role in the accommodation (recuperation?) of significant political dilemmas.[1] Quintessentially, the work of Ricky Gervais in *The Office* creates a difficult and, at times, wholly ambiguous engagement with multiculturalism, where we are left wondering whether the joke is progressive or reactionary. This dilemma yields an important perspective on the emerging social democratic consensus over globalization, that is, the *Third Way*. A fifth chapter picks up previous strands from the 'new satire' to argue that the global financial crisis and the rise of austerity politics provided fertile ground for the return of 'radical comedy'. Here the work of Russell Brand and Stewart Lee is discussed in terms of its ability to question and subvert the dominant mode of market agency: the neoliberal subject. For Brand, this is an opportunity to engage in wider themes of radical democracy, whereas Lee provides a more nuanced deconstruction of our place in global capital/media flows. The sixth chapter will engage with the curious case of *the dog that did not bark* in comic resistances to Brexit. Strangely, for a genre that has so closely associated itself with themes of resistance, British comedy was remarkably aligned with the goal of remaining in Europe, indeed, this uniformity evoked consideration in some quarters as to whether 'liberal comedians' were now a fundamental part of the global capitalist establishment. Finally, the seventh chapter will examine the globalization of British comedy as leading acts now flourish in the US, and their shows are syndicated and distributed globally. The chapter draws discussion to a close by opening up some of the important ethical and political challenges that persist, namely: the question of how to globalize British comedy in terms of race and gender.

---

[1] To be clear, aspects of the comic vernacular routinely draw upon and deploy language that is both problematic and which some may find offensive. This is most obvious in the case of material that uses swear words. Aspects of the theoretical justification for why vulgar language can be an important part of comic resistance are discussed in Chapter 1. While I believe it is important to critique the use of this language within comedy, not least because the subversion and re-signification of such language is precisely a technique of comic resistance, there are some important limits that should be acknowledged. In particular, one line of argument will consider the use of racist language by comedians in order to foreground and question the ethical politics of otherwise resistant humor. Where possible I have tried to use such language sparingly or in footnotes, re-producing it for the purpose of critique.

1

Everyday Comic Resistance
in Global Context

Introduction

While the study of comedy and politics can boast a venerable lineage that spans several disciplines and theoretical approaches, the practice of comic resistance is not normally considered an important subject of *global* politics. Indeed, as the Introduction argued, at least one of the key approaches – the instrumental approach – has understood the political significance of comedy in fundamentally state-centric terms. Although the critical approach raised wider, utopian concerns with truth, emancipation, and 'the people', it had a tendency to read modern manifestations of comedy as either a legitimating or a disciplinary element in modernity and global capitalism. On this view, the resistant potential of comedy was deeply qualified, as likely an ideological smokescreen, or a 'medicinal bath' for docile market subjects. Instead, this book will read comedy as an everyday practice of resistance in global context, where the very idea of resistance is politically productive: part of the generative grammar of global market life.

This chapter will situate comic resistance in global context by engaging the everyday turn in IR and IPE. This literature foregrounds the importance of (apparently) small, mundane, or otherwise marginal actors and practices in global politics (Best and Paterson, 2010; Solomon and Steele, 2017; Elias and Roberts, 2018). Crucial to the everyday turn is the idea that *the agency* of non-elite subjects is far greater than is normally assumed by mainstream approaches to the 'big issues and actors' of the 'international system' (Hobson and Seabrooke, 2007). This can yield a critical position on the politics of globalization whereby a prevailing focus on large states (and their elites), or the structural power of global capitalism, is supplanted by the constitutive agency of everyday market subjects and rationalities (Langley, 2007). On this view, it is not simply that everyday actors and practices are 'added onto' the study of global politics, but that their self-understandings and habits can tell us much about how global politics is 'known', shaped and constructed (Brassett, 2018). In turn, I will argue, the circulation of – *and resistance to* – specific rationalities and discourses of globalization can be refigured as a contingent process located in everyday practices of global politics like comedy.

The chapter proceeds in three sections. Section 1 will engage the everyday turn in IR and IPE. On the one hand, the proliferation of everyday approaches has licensed an expansive empirical concern for new subjects and practices *that matter* in global politics. For some, this has translated into a research focus on the role of 'non-elite' groups and their agency to contest global social power relations (Herod, 2007; Morton, 2007). Equally, there is a growing recognition of the vast range of everyday and cultural practices that shape the politics of globalization. Examples include everyday saving and borrowing (Langley, 2008), carnival art about finance (De Goede, 2005), ethical consumption (Watson, 2007), films about the economy on Netflix (Brassett and Heine, forthcoming), and bingo (Bedford, 2019). On the other hand, and moving beyond empirical expansion, the everyday turn can help to articulate important theoretical dilemmas over the relationship between resistance and power. While some regard 'the everyday' as an attractive and untapped resource that yields multiple new forms of agency in global context, others have framed it as a rather more problematic category, itself a violent spatialization of political life (Davies, 2016). On this view, a critical approach should reflect the layers of colonial, corporate, gendered and racialized power that *produce* 'everyday life' as such, that is, as both *marginal to*, and yet somehow *necessary for* the coherence of global politics.

This tension between viewing the everyday as a resource of resistant agency vs. a critical concern with how the everyday is constituted as such, points to an important ambiguity for thinking about comic resistance. In straightforward terms, addressing the vernacular of comedy must consider how jokes relay, and reproduce – *whether subversively or not* – problematic concepts and stereotypes of race, gender, class and so on. Section 2 will therefore make the case for exploring a performative approach to comic resistance, one which foregrounds the 're-iterative power of discourse to produce what it names' in order to reflect the dilemmas and potentialities of the (satirical) subject (Butler,

1993: 2). While British comedy is a limited and contingent vernacular of everyday resistance, one which often reproduces androcentric, colonial and class-based hierarchies, I will argue that it nevertheless provides a creative realm in which to engage such ambiguities.

What discourses of global politics does British comedy perform? What possibilities and limits does that performance entail? Beyond a critical concern with recuperation, I suggest that the contingent emergence of a vernacular form of British comedy is able to tell a productive *and proliferative* story about market subjectivity in global context. While the precise details of this story will run through the next several chapters, this chapter will attempt to fix ideas through a reading of one prominent example. Section 3 will therefore read the work of Armando Iannucci, and specifically *The Armando Iannucci Shows*, as a keynote example of everyday global resistance.

Against traditional approaches to global resistance that begin (and end) with a logic of opposition – resistance against power, weak vs. strong and so on – an everyday approach foregrounds the dynamic interactions, negotiations and accommodations that go on *within power*. Not that these complex entwinements negate the cause or 'goal' of resistance, but that the small acts of resistance are taken as generative – catalytic even – of (potentially new, more inclusive) social/power relations (Halberstam, 2011). Understanding the everyday qualities of resistance therefore involves apprehending the agency of market subjects *within* globalization. In the work of Iannucci, I argue, comic resistance draws upon *and reproduces* complex understandings of reflective consumption, value-driven production and ethical branding. On this view, the satirical market subject of comedy is a reflective, incisive and self-deprecating soul, whose art of generating laughter can be seen as both *resistant to* and *productive of* globalizing logics. This combines to illustrate the research themes and dilemmas that subsequent chapters will draw out of the history of British comedy more broadly.

1 The everyday turn in global politics

Recent years have seen a growing interest in the role and significance of everyday life in global politics (Best and Paterson, 2010; Guillaume and Huysmans, 2019). A now broad literature has arguably done much to decentre the prevailing theoretical tradition and empirical approaches in IR and IPE, which privilege the role and interests of 'big' actors and processes (Hobson and Seabrooke, 2007). Instead a range of new approaches seek to identify and explore the importance of everyday, non-elite, small, mundane or otherwise marginal actors and processes in global politics. By no means a united or uncontested field, the everyday turn in global politics is nevertheless a significant point of departure for this book. Key debates over the importance and form of everyday resistance, the critical politics of constituting the everyday as such, and the more general opening of global politics to a range of feminist, postcolonial and post-structural theoretical approaches can all help to ground and inform the study of comedy. From the obviously marginal status accorded to humour and joking in many accounts of global politics, to the vexed questions of gender, race and colonial privilege that permeate British comedy, the everyday turn can shed light on how and why 'laughing matters' in global context.

The primary cut of the everyday turn in global politics is to move empirical attention away from the traditional concerns of IR and IPE. Beyond an almost exclusive concern with big states, international organizations, global actors, powerful leaders, and global 'issues areas' of security, cooperation, trade, finance, development and so on, the everyday turn has ushered in a plethora of new subjects and cases. Everyday approaches are often guided by a set of critical theoretical commitments that question the rationalist vision of politics that underpins mainstream ontologies of the 'international system', with its somewhat ahistorical prioritization of the 'interests' of 'the state' (Solomon and Steele, 2017). In particular, feminist scholars have sought to *make sense* of global politics by foregrounding gender structures like patriarchy in order to question the (often invisible) role of women in sustaining – *inter alia* – international diplomacy (and diplomatic men), the sexual demand of military bases and, more broadly, providing domestic work, raising children and so on (Enloe, 2014). Indeed, feminist political economists have highlighted the importance of *social reproduction* in producing, caring for and training a ready supply of labour for the global economy (Bakker, 2007; Elias and Rai, 2018).

A key insight of this literature is to suggest that many of the 'naturalized', common sense images of global politics that are (re)produced in rationalist ontologies of 'the international' are actually dependent upon a set of practices, hierarchies and subordinations that are barely reflected in mainstream theory. When made visible, these 'hierarchies of social difference' can tell a more 'realistic' story about the 'intersectional bases' of power and agency in global politics. Depending on the particular approach taken, an everyday approach might therefore emphasize the role of working-class subjects, gender and racialized hierarchies within and between states, or else various urban/suburban, educated/uneducated, hetero/LGBTQ binaries that structure political agency in global context.

An important contribution of the everyday turn has been to broaden the range of empirical subjects that are consequential in the study of global politics. On the one hand, this growing focus on everyday issues and actors can be part of a constructive effort to describe previously overlooked, yet meaningful or 'causal' stories about global politics. For example, research in IPE has sought to demonstrate the constitutive significance of everyday market subjects, with reference to the growth of popular share ownership, the expansion of homeownership and the related rise of 'entrepreneurial' mortgagors, or the role of gendered assumptions about the 'household budget' in legitimating austerity (Aitken, 2007; Langley, 2007; Brassett and Rethel, 2015). On the other hand, a range of approaches highlight the role of everyday cultural discourses in imagining – *and performing* – global politics per se. In particular, research on popular culture and world politics (PCWP) has celebrated the importance of TV, film, social media, music and other cultural artefacts in shaping public knowledge about – *inter alia* – the politics of migration, everyday ideas about 'terrorist threat', paranoia about Russia as an 'evil empire', and the way video games map target cities as everyday training for future generations of drone pilots (Innes and Topinka, 2017 Grayson 2018; Dean, 2019; Holland, 2019). On this view, it is not so much a question of how the everyday contributes to the mass of objects that 'add up to' global politics, but an orientation to think of the everyday as *a site* of global politics per se.

Broadly speaking, the everyday turn has opened space for thinking about comic resistance in global politics. Thinking in terms of hierarchies of social difference that work through race and class, British comedy has been associated with an important, though often invisible role in legitimating particular structures of inclusion and exclusion (Dodds and Kirby, 2013). Asking the critical question of 'who gets to joke' and 'about what', can yield important insights when focused on sexist and racist jokes that circulate widely in British culture, yet are normally considered a marginal (if regrettable) concern. Yet, in terms of everyday concerns with the agency for resistance, there is clear scope to think about comedy; indeed, that comedy has been associated with the critique and subversion of global discourses of security, neoliberalism, and justice (Brassett, 2009; Amoore and Hall, 2013; Rossdale, 2019). For example, research on terror attacks in the UK has shown how making jokes about the situation, being self-deprecating about the level of 'panic' or 'emergency', as well as satirizing racist or nationalist responses, can all change how the politics of such events is known and experienced (Fox, 2014; Heath-Kelly and Jarvis, 2017). On this view, the everyday politics of comedy chimes with the literature on popular culture that treats it as a site for the 'exchange, negotiation, resistance, and incorporation' of significant global discourses (Grayson et al, 2009: 56). Taken together, there appears to be a strong set of reasons for thinking about everyday practices of comic resistance in global politics; that humour and joking might play a role in concealing – and therefore affirming – consequential hierarchies of social difference in global politics. Or else, the potential for relief and subversion in comedy might allow space to re-think the possibilities for everyday resistance in global politics.

Ambiguities of everyday resistance

If the everyday turn in global politics does much to ground (and justify) an empirical study of comedy, there are important theoretical ambiguities that arise over the question of resistance. In particular, a number of authors have identified how the everyday is often thought of as a space that is virtually synonymous with agency for resistance (Bleiker, 2000; Guillaume, 2011; Davies, 2016). For instance, Hobson and Seabrooke (2007: 16–17) foreground the capacity of everyday actors to 'resist' wider structures of power in global politics. Although the 'actors concerned may not know that they are contributing to change in the local, national, regional or global contexts' (Hobson and Seabrooke, 2007: 18), they can nevertheless be understood as bottom-up drivers of change. This draws from Scott's book: *Weapons of the Weak: Everyday Forms of Peasant Resistance* (1987) and his argument that everyday acts of dissent or refusal are an important element in the social relations of subordinate groups. For Scott, everyday resistance is quiet, dispersed or disguised. Indeed, he identified it with certain common behaviours of the subaltern groups he studied: foot-dragging, sarcasm, passivity, laziness, misunderstandings, disloyalty and so on. Such 'weapons of the weak', he argued, were both a worthy subject of study and an important corollary in wider practices of 'public' resistance. Indeed, despite his celebration of everyday forms of resistance, Scott continuously emphasized the 'potential' for the everyday to connect with 'larger' agendas:

> One day you will be called upon to break a big law in the name of justice and rationality. Everything will depend on it. You have to be ready. How are you going to prepare for that day when it really matters? You have to stay 'in shape' so that when the big day comes you will be ready. What you need is 'anarchist calisthenics.' Every day or so

break some trivial law that makes no sense, even if it's only jaywalking. Use your own head to judge whether a law is just or reasonable. That way, you'll keep trim; and when the big day comes, you'll be ready. (2012: 4–5)

Scott brings a dynamic and practice-oriented understanding to the study of resistance that foregrounds lived experiences. On some occasions, we might require a certain attitude, or 'sly civility', on others it might be gossip or piss-taking that forms the best available 'habit' or 'routine' to draw upon in manifesting resistance. In this way, Scott's logic of practice centres the resister as the primary judge of what to resist, not some universal theory. This is a productive account of everyday resistance that can lend some important methodological purchase to the study of comic resistance. However, despite the attractiveness of this approach to everyday resistance, we should not ignore the potential limitations in this concept of the everyday. In figuring the everyday and everyday resistance in terms of 'non-elite' agency there is a problematic move to accept the 'everyday' as an 'ordinary' or 'natural' category. Scott has been criticized for applying too strong a distinction between the dominant and the subaltern, so that the role of resistance is over-emphasized at the expense of a more nuanced understanding of power relations. Such a view might ignore the role of 'survival' or 'self-discipline' in everyday power relations, or indeed, the capacity for resistance by 'elites' (Chandra, 2015). Indeed, this dilemma can speak directly to the study of comedy.

On one level, there is sometimes a mood to romanticize resistance, whereby empirical and theoretical work can focus on the resistance practices of particular people or groups, *which we favour* (Vintaghen and Johansson, 2013). In terms of comedy, there is a pronounced tendency in the literature to identify and study comic resistance in explicitly normative terms, that is, insofar as it supports the political cause of the marginal and those disposed 'against' the hegemonic (Brassett, 2016). As the critical approach discussed in the Introduction suggests, there are manifold reasons to question how humour and comedy also support conservative, reactionary or fascist political agendas; not least through the related social functions of ragging, humiliation and/or shaming.

On another level, however, it is important to consider what is going on in this move to prioritize the everyday itself. Does a turn to focus on the everyday 'invert', *rather than problematize*, the apparent separation between the global and the everyday? This is a crucial question for thinking about comic resistance, because it fundamentally destabilizes the idea that 'everyday resistance' is important insofar as it 'connects to' larger public resistances. Such an incremental image could thus work to obscure the politics of the everyday, its history and ongoing violence. For Matt Davies (2016), we should instead question how the 'everyday' is produced as an unproblematic site in the first place: as something which is 'simply there', operating in some (usually subservient) relation to the 'global'. Instead, the everyday should be a critical concept, one which invites reflection on the (imperial) politics of producing such normalized categories in the first place. As he argues: 'examining the mutually constitutive relationships between the spatialities and temporalities of the everyday and of contemporary international power relations made possible by colonial practices is the most important contribution a turn to the everyday can make to IPE' (Davies, 2016: 23). Thus, the 'everyday' is not simply 'below' the global – as in popular ideas of 'bottom-up' resistance – but is a critical element in its political production. By way of illustration, Davies points to how 'supermarkets' operate within the everyday lived experiences of cities. While the pristine, air-conditioned aisles provide a calm serene experience for shoppers as they browse their consumption choices, the political reality of supermarkets is of land appropriation and social rupture. As Davies (2016: 33) argues:

> [w]hole ways of life are disrupted as 'supermarkets and shopping centres' ... displace small shops, local service providers, or 'informal' economies and the space defined through the former become enclosures where non-consuming or non-employment 'public' activities are excluded. These are ... everyday but nonetheless violent processes ...

By foregrounding this political history of the everyday, we can begin to reflect its deep imbrications with violent and colonial practices of global politics. When this political history of the everyday is articulated as a critique of everyday comic resistance, we must remain sensitive to the role of humour in speaking/legitimating the vernacular logics of empire, identity and race. Indeed, the next section will argue that this is a crucial ambiguity in the politics of comedy. While certain jokes can reveal the instability and violence of nation or gender, say, others can serve to entrench such exclusionary tropes through stereotype or humiliation. Such ambiguities are part of the politics of everyday comic resistance; they are an acute question of ethics and agency in global politics that should be identified and engaged.

2 Towards a performative politics of comic resistance

While the everyday turn in global politics opens up space for the study of British comedy as a practice of resistance, the previous section identified some important dilemmas. Optimism over the everyday as a site of agency for resistance should be tempered by sensitivity to the disciplinary politics of everyday life, whether through the repetition of gender norms, the racialized valorization of particular languages (and not others), or the self-soothing potential of irony to suggest the nation is suitably reflexive. Further, the spatial politics of everyday life, which is often understood as marginal to (some pre-existing realm of) the global, should be fundamentally historicized through attention to discourses and practices of 'making' the everyday as such. On this view, the apparent valorization of everyday resistance can be problematized insofar it naturalizes ideas of (global) space, the subject and discourse. Does comic resistance question prevailing discourses of global politics? When satirical practices are circulated – *and applauded* – do they lose their subversive potential? Such questions infer deep imbrications between resistance and power, and between discourse and subject. That is to say, the satirical market subject always-already speaks 'a language'; everyday comic resistance *works within power*, and not as some easy corrective *pace* the instrumental approach, that is, 'joking for our side'. Instead, there is an ongoing *politics of* resistance:

> power and resistance are not the dichotomous phenomenon that is often implied. In practical interactions they are mixed and interconnected hybrids. Agents of resistance often simultaneously promote power-loaded discourses, being the bearers of hierarchies and stereotypes as well as of change. Hence, each actor is both the subject and the object of power – the subject is exposed to the ranking and stereotyping as well as promoting repressive 'truths' – thus being both an agent exercising powers and a subaltern who has been subjugated and reduced to order by disciplinary strategies. Resistance is always situated, in a context, a historic tradition, a certain place and/or social space forged by those who rebel. And even, not to say especially, when resistance is innovative, experimental and creative, it needs to build on the material left by other rebels – stories, myths, symbols, structures and tools available in that special situation ... (Vintaghen and Johanssen, 2013: 14)

On this view, attention can be directed to the language and the form of British comedy; the everyday vernacular of resistance and the various stories, myths and tools it produces over time. Appreciating the contingency, indeed the violence of a particular language or practice of resistance, does not *require us* to dispense with the mode or form of resistance. In particular, if such a practice of resistance is persistent over time, it might actually suggest a greater ethical responsibility to engage it; not least in order to understand the nature and effects of its repetition (Brassett, 2009). In the case of British comedy, I will argue, the progressive formation of a satirical subject that is reflexive to its own contingent position in everyday global discourses, can suggest an important politics of engagement that is routinely overlooked in the prevailing approaches. In short, there is a performative politics of comic resistance.

A performative approach to comic resistance takes seriously the dual potential of jokes to both critique and affirm power relations. The point is that this potential is contingent, indeed subject to further performances, which might circulate in new or unexpected ways. As the Introduction described, resistance is less as an 'opposition to' power, and more like a productive practice of self-making; in Foucauldian terms, a 'care of the self' (Foucault, 1990). For Foucault, the idea of resistance was never about an escape from, or an overcoming of power relations, but was instead a question of re-fashioning the subject *within* power, that 'the will not to be governed is always the will not to be governed *thusly*, like that, by these people, at this price' (Foucault, 2007: 75). Indeed, Judith Butler extends this idea to argue that the subject retains the potential for a kind of *poiesis*. Again, not that this implies a fully autonomous self-making agent, but that it is part of the play of the subject with(in) the conditions of its subjectivity:

> This work on the self ... takes place within the context of a set of norms that precede and exceed the subject. These are invested with power and recalcitrance, setting limits to what will be considered to be an intelligible formation of the subject within a given historical scheme of things. There is no making of oneself outside of a mode of subjectivation and hence no self-making outside of the norms that orchestrate the possible forms that a subject may take. (Butler, 2005: 17)

From this perspective, the question of everyday resistance is less about 'opposing' a systemic rationality of globalization, and more about understanding the intimate entwinement between historical context – (which includes markets, but also culture, race, gender and so on) – and the subject. Resistance is thus a performative practice; as central to the making of power relations as it is to their re-imagination over time.

On this view, my approach to everyday comic resistance can fully reflect the potentials identified by previous scholars of comedy and politics like Bakhtin (1984) and Orwell (1945). In particular, they identify the visceral qualities in laughter and vulgarity that give comedy its vernacular power to resonate with wider audiences. Indeed, Orwell (1945) read into these capacities a potential purpose, indeed morality, which is important to grasp:

> A joke is a temporary rebellion against virtue, and its aim is not to degrade the human being but to remind him that he is already degraded. A willingness to make extremely obscene jokes can co-exist with very strict moral standards, as in Shakespeare. Some comic writers, like Dickens, have a direct political purpose, others, like Chaucer or Rabelais, accept the corruption of society as something inevitable.

But, as the Introduction suggested, it would be a mistake to reify such purpose, or indeed the larger critical function of laughter identified by Bakhtin (1984), as some objective or universal quality in comic resistance (that is of necessity betrayed). Instead, we need to take account of the contingency and instability of subversion, that resistance and recuperation are part of the conversation, so to speak. As Butler argues:

> I am not interested in delivering judgements on what distinguishes the subversive from the unsubversive. Not only do I believe that such judgements cannot be made out of context, but that they cannot be made in ways that endure through time ('contexts' are themselves posited unities that undergo temporal change and expose their essential disunity). Just as metaphors lose their metaphoricity as they congeal through time into concepts, so subversive performances always run the risk of becoming deadening cliches through their repetition and, most importantly, through their repetition within commodity culture where 'subversion' carries market value. The effort to name the criterion for subversiveness will always fail, and ought to. (Butler, 1999: xxii)

The everyday practice of comic resistance is thus a 'live issue', which carries a potential for 'rebellion', yet also struggles with commodification. Rather than seek to judge whether a joke is 'correctly resistant', a performative approach is concerned with what comic resistance 'does'; how it circulates and 'congeals' over time. Just as Vintaghen and Johanssen reflect on the 'stories myths and symbols' that are available for future rebels, a focus on comedy requires sensitivity to the kinds of techniques that are established for future satirists to re-work.

The chapters that follow will therefore argue that the context and performances of specific British comedians and satirists have given rise to a vernacular of everyday resistance in global context. This vernacular both draws upon and decentres its targets (of empire, hubris, class, race, gender and so on), while providing a critical, visceral and creative set of 'stories', 'myths' and 'tools' for new comic subjects to work with(in). In that vein, the next section will tease out elements of this argument by locating the methodological orientation of the book: to read the performative politics of comic resistance through the work of specific comedians.

3 Subversion and failure in the work of Armando Iannucci

In everyday terms, the capacity of humour to be obscene, vulgar, smutty and so on, is an important element its ability to 'communicate' with wider audiences. As Simon Critchley (2002: 87) argues, 'the genius of jokes is that they light up the common features of our world, not by offering theoretical considerations or by writing two admirably fat volumes of Habermas's *The Theory of Communicative Action*, but in a more practical way. They are forms of practical abstraction, socially embedded philosophizing.' Humour can thus play an edifying role, providing a space to reflect on issues that might otherwise be excluded from public discourse. Elsewhere, Critchley (1999: 120) channels Bakhtin to celebrate the visceral qualities of laughter:

> Laughter is a convulsive movement, it is like sobbing or like an orgasm, it is involuntary, it sometimes even hurts. It is contagious and solidaristic – think of the intersubjective dimensions of giggling, particularly when it concerns something obscene. In this way, perhaps, we might say that laughter in its solidaristic dimension has an ethical function insofar as the simple sharing of a joke recalls what is shared

in our lifeworld practices, not in a heroic way, but more quietly and discreetly.

Indeed, for Critchley (1999: 120), this is a vision of comedy that anticipates an everyday politics of global capitalism, disturbing the naturalized experiences of consumer culture, laughter as a 'site of resistance to the alleged total administration of society, a node of non-identity in the idealizing rage of commodification'. Rather than functioning as just an escape from the world, comedy can be instructive, cathartic, democratic, even.

Again, while performative approaches are unlikely to name or specify a universally valid element of comic resistance in this way, they nevertheless offer some clues. Although comedy is not regarded as a universal 'delivery vessel' for truth or democracy – *pace* the critical approach – or as a straightforward resistance against power *pace* the instrumental approach – it can potentially serve as an embodiment of the contingency and instability of meaning at the heart of performance. Quintessentially, Judith Butler looks at drag as a form of subversion, arguing that in 'imitating gender, drag implicitly reveals the imitative structure of gender itself – as well as its contingency' (1990: 187). While such subversion is momentary and fleeting, indeed, subject to recuperation within capitalist culture, it introduces an important way of thinking about comic resistance through drag:

> In place of the law of heterosexual coherence, we see sex and gender denaturalized by means of a performance which avows their distinctness and dramatizes the cultural mechanism of their fabricated unity. (1990: 187–8)

Instead, of a clear joke that delivers a punchline – although there may be many such jokes in a drag act – the drag artist enters into a communicative relationship with the audience; meanings are emphasized and de-emphasized, stereotypes are embraced, ridiculousness celebrated. Indeed, this 'live element' in comedy is an important recognition of the implicit dialogue that can emerge; that the audience is very often a productive element in the comedic interaction. On this view, the performance of jokes can be catalytic of subversive thoughts; bodily reactions in the viewer subject go some way to embrace the visceral qualities of laughter as *potentially* resistant. Indeed, this productive politics of subversion is something that Jack Halberstam has developed through the concept of 'failure' and its capacity to performatively destabilize the everyday subjects and rationalities of neoliberalism:

29

> Under certain circumstances failing, losing, forgetting, unmaking, undoing, unbecoming, not knowing may in fact offer more creative, more cooperative, more surprising ways of being in the world. Failing is something queers do and have always done exceptionally well; for queers failure can be a style, to cite Quentin Crisp, or a way of life, to cite Foucault, and it can stand in contrast to the grim scenarios of success that depend on 'trying and trying again'. (Halberstam, 2011: 3)

Failure here, is not some interactive outcome through which we might 'learn to improve', but an 'art' of self-making subjects who perform and reflect upon the contingency of their experience. Thus, I would argue, if the everyday is to also function as a critical concept, then it must take account of the way it emerges through particular forms that suit (underpin?) global relations of power. Is this something that comic resistance can perform? Halberstam (2011: 4–5) reads the film *Little Miss Sunshine* as an (inspirational) example of how *comic failure* can articulate a form of resistance to neoliberal globalization through a subversion of everyday family life:

> With her porn-obsessed junky grandfather providing her with the choreography for her pageant routine and a cheerleading squad made up of her gay suicidal uncle, a Nietzsche reading mute brother, and aspiring but flailing motivational speaker father and an exasperated stay-at-home mom, Olive is destined to fail, and fail spectacularly. But while her failure could be a source of misery and humiliation, and while it does indeed deliver precisely this, it also leads to a kind of ecstatic exposure of the contradictions of a society obsessed with meaningless competition.

Halberstam argues that such moments, of 'ecstatic exposure', might lead to a 'new kind of optimism', that would eschew 'positive thinking', and allow for an appreciation of how things hang together: 'a little ray of sunshine that produces shade and light in equal measure and knows that the meaning of one always depends on the meaning of the other' (Halberstam, 2011: 5). On this view, I will argue, the practice of comic resistance can – *but does not necessarily* – disturb the 'assumed coherence' between the everyday and the global. Halberstam's example works by exposing the violent ordering of the everyday 'through' self-help and positive thinking, the way it produces subjects and rationalities of the family, which become ridiculous through repeated and overlapping failures. In the example below, I will explore a comparable form of subversion that operates in the work of Armando Iannucci and his satirical reflections on the (ethical) self. In particular, I will argue that his various considerations of 'failure' can be productive of critical lines of thought on the coherence of the global market subject, and the everyday hierarchies of gender, consumerism and 'ethics', indeed 'Britishness', which structure it.

The market life of failure

Armando Iannucci is a prolific comedy writer and producer, who has been involved with some of the most important and influential British satires. While later chapters in this book will look to his more successful shows like *The Day Today* and *The Thick of It*, this section will focus on his comparatively less well-known series: *The Armando Iannucci Shows*. I will argue that these shows crystallize some central themes in his comedy – the existential emptiness of the market self, the pomposity of mediatized society, and a painful masculine self-doubt. Indeed, the opening episode – 'Twats' – deals with Armando's worry that he might look like a twat in front of other people. He is unable to play football and lives in fear that a ball might one day stray off a pitch and the players will ask him to kick it back. He therefore adjusts his running routes to go *away* from football pitches, recounting: "it was the same for Seb Coe".[1] In another scene, he finds it difficult to talk with other men, struggling on the rudimentary basics of football. He tries to make do by deploying casually racist ideas like blindfolding "all the foreign players" (to make it more interesting). He later misunderstands a discussion about 4-4-2 tactics, criticizing the strategic formation because foreign players have "all the skills", so you can just stick them anywhere and they know what to do.[2]

Armando worries about what people think of him, whether or not he's funny, and whether everyone knows something that they are not telling him. Indeed, the show presents his interior monologue that splices different anxieties as he goes about his daily life – "this is the bit I hate, taking my car to the garage, I know nothing about cars.... Every time a mechanic comes out from under my car I feel like a little

---

[1] *The Armando Iannucci Shows*, episode 1, 'Twats', 30 August 2001, https://www.youtube.com/watch?v=oZdrVo8ERyQ (accessed 2 May 2020).

[2] Ibid.

slug, who's just handed him a piece of lettuce saying: can you cut it up for me please?" – as scenes of a mechanic criticizing his car play out, Armando begs him to take his money, and openly asks: "help me?"[3] But on entering the garage, Armando is more worried about his own behaviour – thinking he acted like a real "jizz head at that party last night" and worrying about "that guy", who everyone thinks is really funny, and that he could never be that funny. As these thoughts are running, Armando arrives in the reception area of the mechanics, where the head mechanic is informing one of his customers – who also knows nothing about cars – that there is "a bit of a problem with your card. It says you're a twat."[4] Despite the customer's protestations, "It says it here, he's a twat!" (he points to the till display). Another mechanic suggests they "check the list" of "local twats operating in the area" – and they are pleased to find a photo of him there. When the customer eventually leaves they focus on Armando, as his interior monologue now wonders if his clothes make him look 'a bit gay'. The mechanics see him and accuse him of being a twat. Armando runs out wearing S&M gear:

> 'I'm not a twat, other people are! Those people at weddings who are served champagne but say 'its sparkling wine actually', they're twats, that man there, he's the sort who says 'cheer up it might never happen', twat. People who ring up Radio 5 to argue with Nicky Campbell, twats. That man I saw on the regional news, every year he writes a song for Princess Anne's birthday, he's been doing it for 16 years [Man singing song about Princess Anne with accordion] – *He was the biggest twat!*'[5]

In this way, Iannucci presents a reflective, self-critical dilemma regarding *the failing self*, often in mundane, market situations, that is, down the pub, or with the mechanics. It carries the vulgarity and obscenity emphasized in the previous section, but it foregrounds a reflexive discourse, always wondering about the 'awkward fit' between the self and society. Aspects of this reflect a general sense of doubt, wrapped up in a form of 1990s irony that will be discussed in later chapters. But the way Iannucci develops the joke allows for a wider questioning of market life, from questions of how to be a man, when masculinity

---

[3]   Ibid.
[4]   Ibid.
[5]   Ibid.

has become commodified through football and cars, to wider issues developed in the episode 'Morality',[6] which asks questions about how to be a moral consumer, and how to think about humanitarian aid.

In the opening sketch a group of TV producers strike a deal with a Buddhist monastery to do a reality TV show, where monks compete to be the "least materialistic" and the "most spiritual" – the show is a success and the TV producers conga to the chant "we're good at telly, we're good as telly".[7] In another sketch, some managers at a quarry company realize they only have one order for their rocks, it comes from the Saudi Arabian government, which wants to use the rock for public stoning ceremonies – worried, they ask: "Will the company logo be visible?"[8] In another scene, Armando is unsure about how to express his moral self via various consumer choices, when "buying an aerosol is an atrocity" because most of Lapland will be destroyed, but it's ok because "if I buy two, then I get this free cassette, which will destroy the live music industry".[9] Indeed, as morality is increasingly reduced to individual choices, Armando fixates on how to show he's a good person; he doesn't want to give money to a beggar because it will "go to his pimp", but Armando returns the next day to show him an old picture of him once being kind to children.[10] Relatedly, his interior monologue is concerned that, in the old days, you could tell who the "bad guy" was on the news, because they came out of a police station with a bag on their head with crowds shouting at them – an observation that is juxtaposed with a scene of a baying mob chasing him down the street because of his poor consumer choices.[11] This discussion of the moral consumer self in market life then segues to a discussion on global aid:

	[a Kenyan village, generic ethnic music playing]
Mafuna:	My name is Mafuna. This is my Kenyan homeland. We live on the plains by the edge of the desert. Though we are busy day and night tending our cattle and irrigating our fields, we have heard a cry for help from far away. In

---

[6]   *The Armando Iannucci Shows*, episode 6, 'Morality', 11 October 2001 https://www.youtube.com/watch?v=fWsPW_KrIDM (accessed 2 May 2020).

[7]   Ibid.

[8]   Ibid.

[9]   Ibid.

[10]   Ibid.

[11]   Ibid.

Britain, the home of theatre, the Bristol Old Vic is close to bankruptcy. London venues like the Garrick and the Royal Court receive next to no funding and people are unwilling to pay more than twenty pounds a ticket to see contemporary drama.

[now in a theatre district]

Mafuna: In London desperate people like Harold Pinter, no longer have the chance to say challenging things about the human condition. Most of the waiters here are out of work actors, forced to serve risottos because they cannot get decent parts.

[Kenyan family watching an awards ceremony on TV]

Child: Who is that man, mother?

Mother: It is Simon Callow. He is wretched.

Mafuna: What use is rice to Trevor Nunn? What he needs is our money! My people have been busy raising money for this vital cause. Sponsored voice projection classes, and the wearing of ruffs, are two ways we are trying to help. My cousin Paul has been sponsored to till his entire field before dusk. [Paul is dressed in a rabbit costume]

Village Children (cheer): Zoe Wannamaker, WE LOVE YOU!!

Mafuna: We are rebuilding our homes with cravats and making Masai shields to defend the future of talented actresses.

[with actors sitting around him]

Mafuna: Imagine a world where there are no plays where a barn is used as a metaphor for Anglo-Irish relations. Since coming here, I've seen two of these plays and I've started to really think differently about things. Haven't I?

Actors (cheer): YES![12]

---

[12] Ibid.

Conclusion: The productivity of comic resistance?

In conclusion, 'Theatre Aid' is in an interesting place to *start* thinking about the politics of British comedy. The joke plays on a reversal: the (at the time) prevalent mood of humanitarian concern expressed by celebrity activism like Live Aid and Comic Relief is taken as the target. Instead of a rich Northern celebrity, the principal is a young Kenyan boy, Mafuna, who, despite living a largely peasant lifestyle, has heard of the plight of the Old Vic and its dwindling funds. Thus, Kenyans must save British actors from servitude. However, in reversing the subject positions of global humanitarianism the joke is also about the form. Mafuna travels to witness the plight of the actors, and the plays make him think differently, much as Comic Relief sends comedians to dig trenches and experience the 'warmth' of communal feeling in Kenya. As a result, the humanitarian narrative of intimacy or solidarity is established, so that we believe the Kenyan village 'knows' (or 'has learned') something about the actors they are saving. In full fundraising mode, the Kenyan village is visibly adorned with signs like 'Keep Dame Judy Dench Alive!' and 'We're all deeply interested in subtext'.[13]

In these ways, I would argue that 'Theatre Aid' can serve as important example of everyday comic resistance in global context. A clear central joke that allows several iterations and layers in a short (3-minute) sequence, yes, but also, a challenging movement that asks fundamental questions about global context, human relations and the wider politics of global ethics. The privileged, indeed, imperial position of humanitarian sympathy is an important, if uncomfortable, point of reflection. The fact that such critical ideas are communicated through a popular, everyday form of entertainment, suggests a capacity for wide public engagement with complex questions about neocolonial power relations. On this view, British comedy has a 'potential' to resist the ethical and political hubris that can legitimate violent global practices.

From this short illustration, I hope to firm up some of theoretical and methodological framework that will guide the chapters that follow. A productive politics of comic resistance is far from 'pure', indeed the gendered and racialized politics of Iannucci speaks of a highly ambiguous, unstable, performance; one that crafts (the question of) a 'permissible' form of agency in an everyday global context of intersectional violence. Indeed, the upper-class, English, white, male make-up of British comedy will be a subject that will be returned to

---

[13] Ibid.

several times in subsequent chapters. But even – *or especially* – within the context of such ambiguities, the everyday resistances of British comedy can offer productive insights on how global politics is 'known', 'contested', 'inhabited' and 'lived'. There is an ecstatic exposure, a performative failure by Armando to reconcile his self with the everyday discipline of global rationalities of masculinity or morality. In short, the everyday politics of comic resistance can animate and subvert the rationalities and subjectivities of globalization.

2

The Satire Boom: Imperial Decline and the Rise of the Everyday Elite

Introduction

The origins of the 'satire boom' in 1950s Britain might seem curious. While the end of the Second World War brought relief (and the good fortune of victory), the nation had to adapt to some stark realities. The war had been costly, in human and economic terms. At the same time, the superior wealth and power of the US served as a demonstration of the changing position of Britain in global politics. The US was a former colony, and just as it reached preponderance, there were a growing number of national independence movements turning against British rule. The rise to popularity of satire happened during a period of acute decline, loss of political self-confidence and protracted self-analysis. As Stuart Ward (2001a: 12) argues: 'Ideas about British "character" ... became difficult to sustain as the external prop of the imperial world was progressively weakened. Notions of duty, service, loyalty, deference, stoic endurance and self-restraint and gentlemanly conduct were insidiously undermined by the steady erosion of the imperial edifice.'

Thinking about the satire boom as an everyday practice of resistance must therefore reflect and engage this politics of imperial decline; part of the cultural negotiation of this erosion of global power. Domestically, the late 1940s and early 1950s saw the implementation of austerity policies, many which went further than war-time rationing (Carpenter, 2000: 4–5). Internationally, this once 'great' and 'proud nation' that had been victorious in the 'two world wars', now faced palpable questions – both military and moral – about how to maintain global influence, a problematic that crystallized with the Suez crisis (Carpenter, 2000: 9–11). Widely seen as a national humiliation, Suez underlined how the politics of imperial decline would unfold in ways that fundamentally questioned the self-identity of British political culture, with its confidence, deference and *bloody mindedness*. Again, why did the 'satire boom' happen during this period? What was it about the combination of austerity and imperial decline that created so much (demand for) comedy? What is the 'global' significance of this growing British interest in humour, wit and irony?

This chapter will locate these questions via an analysis of the everyday politics of the satire boom. Those involved are often held up as the finest generation of comedians that Britain has produced, and their oeuvre marks out an avowedly resistant and critical mobilization of irony, where the satirizing of (all) political figures and a generalized subversion of 'British' values and hierarchies laid the groundwork for subsequent iterations of the comic vernacular (Brassett, 2009). Understanding the satire boom in terms of everyday comic resistance can help to situate the work of shows like *Beyond the Fringe* and *Monty Python* – as well as the satirical news formats of *That Was The Week That Was* (*TW3*) and *Private Eye* – in a wider set of global social power relations. Beyond instrumental concerns with the political economy of the 'arched eyebrow business' and the apparent 'selling out' of satirical principles (Wagg, 1996: 340–3), I will argue that a performative approach can yield important insights on the transformation in everyday experiences of, and political agency *to engage*, global politics.

In short, the satire boom produced a new set of subjects and rationalities through which global politics could be understood, contested and changed. Satires of British politics were inner directed, playing on a profound dissonance between the imperial self-identity of establishment elites and the stark reality of imperial decline; an ongoing – if sometimes repressed – humiliation. Sketches about the heroic myth of war, the venality of judges, and a grotesquerie of 'Upper Class Twits' or the men at the Ministry of Silly Walks suggested both a resistance to the 'establishment' as well as a new-found confidence to explore the individualism and social liberation of the time. The performance of this critical language was simultaneously a critique and an embodiment of wider changes in global political economy: the rise of mass media news and entertainment, as well as a growing rupture between an increasingly cherished private sphere and an 'invasive' public politics, which crystallized in debates over the 'permissive society' (Wagg, 2002). Yet, the productive point is that these performances circulated, *and still circulate*, in a manner that places self-deprecation and irony at the heart of national self-identity.

The new language of comic resistance carried a critical potential to reflect on/within global politics. Rather than a sop or a comfort blanket, the ironic disposition of satire enabled – *indeed valorized* – a language, a form, that sought to 'prick pomposity' in (and through) the everyday life of global politics. While many debates on the satire boom are focused on the ambiguities entailed in performing comic resistance from a position of relative social and cultural privilege, I will argue that the circulation of satire, its popularity as a new form of media entertainment, and the performance of self-deprecation as a social ideal, all carry important implications for thinking about *what is left behind*. In terms of the literature on everyday politics, this can be framed as a question of how bottom-up cultural changes drive or legitimate an emergent social consensus. Yet it also illustrates how comic resistance is not simply a movement 'against' power, but also a productive enactment of those very global social power relations. On this view, the satire boom provided a new basis of confidence, an 'ontological security' that irony and self-deprecation could 'take on board' the decline (and excess) of empire, while performing a 'boldness-to-reflect' about/within global politics (Brassett et al, forthcoming).

This argument is developed over three sections. Section 1 introduces some of the most significant and avowedly resistant work of this new generation of satirists. It focuses on the subversion of establishment hubris, and how this proliferated a range of ethical and social critiques of – *inter alia* – class, gender and religion. Section 2 foregrounds certain ambiguities in the satire boom, which arguably qualify its resistant potentials. In particular, it reflects the class and gender privilege of the comedians themselves; the marginalization of women and problematic satires of race; as well as the pronounced business acumen of its protagonists. Then section 3 identifies some important potentialities in the performative politics of satire, how it fostered a certain sensibility to expand the scope of political reflection in comedy, beyond a politics of 'elites' to a politics of the 'social' and 'cultural' nuances of the everyday.

1 Satirical resistance: empire, class and the self

Situating the satire boom in global context involves a basic comic insight that the 'set-up' for any joke is crucial to the payoff. The global context that Britain faced was political-economic decline and the need to negotiate a new consensus (Gamble, 1994). A new common sense would need to be negotiated between a ruling class that inhabited the old establishment ideas of deference and imperial responsibility, on the one hand, and a newly emergent mass society that was embracing individualism and liberal experimentalism, on the other. In a word, the old order often appeared quite silly to the new. As Stuart Ward summarizes:

> the end of empire and the steady diminution of British power and prestige ... became the source of immense laughter and ridicule. The ever widening gap between the global reach of British national aspirations and the encroaching external realities of the post-war world provided new avenues for comic exploration of the imperial ethos and the myth of Britain's 'world role'. (Ward, 2001b: 91)

If the old order was dying, then the new order found it all terribly funny. Quintessentially, the impersonation of Harold Macmillan by Peter Cook in *Beyond the Fringe* went to the heart of the global context of imperial decline, portraying an intimate lampoon of a Conservative Prime Minister as he sought to navigate changing times:

> 'Good evening. I have recently been travelling around the world, on your behalf, and at your expense, visiting some of the chaps with whom I hope to be shaping your future. I went first to Germany, and there I spoke with the German Foreign Minister, Herr ... Herr and there, and we exchanged many frank words in our respective languages; so precious little came of that in the way of understanding. I would, however, emphasize, that the little that did come of it was indeed truly precious.
>
> I then went to America, and there I had talks with the young vigorous President of that great country, and danced with his very lovely lady wife. We talked of many things, including Great Britain's position in the world as some kind of honest broker. I agreed with him, when he said that no nation could be more honest; and he agreed with me, when I chaffed him, and said that *no nation could be broker*.... This type of genial, statesmanlike banter often went on late into the night.' (Cook, see Wilmut, 1980: 18–19)

The form of this joke touches on a number of weak spots in British self-identity: ignorance, arrogance and weakness. It foregrounds the body of the Prime Minister, including his limitations with language; the everyday nature of political address with its vague condescension, and the playful, yet loaded barb that 'no nation could be broker'. Indeed, the personal nature of the address is set in a sharp juxtaposition with some of the 'larger' themes of global security, which he goes on to discuss:

> 'Our talks ranged over a wide variety of subjects including that of the Skybolt missile programme. And after a great deal of good-natured give and take I decided on behalf of Great Britain to accept Polaris in place of Skybolt. This is a good solution because, as far as I can see, the Polaris starts where the Skybolt left off. In the sea.
>
> 'I was privileged to see some actual photographs of this weapon. The President was kind enough to show me actual photographs of this missile, beautiful photographs taken by the Karsh of Ottawa. A very handsome weapon, we shall be very proud to have them, the photographs that is, we don't get the missile until around 1970 – in the meantime we shall just have to keep our fingers crossed, sit very quietly, and *try not to alienate anyone.*
>
> 'This is not to say we do not have our own Nuclear Striking Force – we do, we have the Blue Steel, a very effective missile, as it has a range of one hundred and fifty miles, which means we can just about get Paris – *and by God we will.*' (Cook, see Wilmut, 1980: 19)

On the one hand, this kind of genial self-deprecation of 'Great' Britain can be understood to perform a playful sense of irony, where the body of the Prime Minister is the focus for the wider, existential realities of decline.[1] Indeed, despite the effectiveness of the impression, Peter Cook maintained that he actually held Macmillan in high esteem, attributing any satirical 'power' to the fact that it was 'the first time for several years that a living Prime Minister had been impersonated on the stage' (see Wilmut, 1980: 18). On this view, the satire of imperial bloody mindedness – "we can just about get Paris ... *and by God we will*" – is affectionate joshing. On the other hand, and despite the political

---

[1] In one interview, Peter Miller recounted: "I think one of the things that characterised our 'so called' satire was that it was actually quite amiable, it wasn't bitter, nihilistic satire, it was just amused, cynical, sarcastic, but actually in some strange way, half in love with the thing that it attacked." Cited from *Heroes of Comedy: Peter Cook*, 19 January 1998, https://www.youtube.com/watch?v=X-MOhn3MeOQ (accessed 4 May 2020).

sympathies of Cook, the routine also portrayed a more critical sense shared by many fans: that there was something implicitly 'left-wing' about this new form of comedy. Indeed, as it went on:

> 'While I was abroad, I was very moved to receive letters from people in acute distress all over the country. And one in particular, from an old age pensioner in Fyfe, is indelibly printed on my memory. Let me read it to you. It reads, "Dear Prime Minister, I am an old age pensioner in Fyfe, living on a fixed income of some two pounds, seven shillings a week. This is not enough. What do you of the Conservative Party propose to do about it?" [He tears the letter up] Well let me say right away, Mrs McFarlane – as one Scottish old age pensioner to another – be of good cheer. There are many people in this country today who are far worse off than yourself. And it is the policy of the Conservative Party to see that this position is maintained.'
> (Cook, see Wilmut, 1980: 19)

Whether the 'satire boom' actually was 'left wing' or not, is debatable. With hindsight, it might be possible to discern in Cook's monologue the model of anti-Tory satire, which later became central to alternative and radical comedy. However, at the time, the primary cut came through the personification of power, and the plurality of subjects and political viewpoints targeted in other sketches suggests there was no sustained political agenda. Instead, a politician, the Prime Minister, was being joshed, teased, in public, and audiences enjoyed it. *Beyond the Fringe* rose quickly from university review, through the Edinburgh Fringe, to conquer the West End and then 'America'. Deference to power and hierarchy was not only weakening, but its transgression through satire was easily sold. From the BBC commissioning the highly successful *TW3*, which pioneered the satirical news format to an audience of around 10 million, to private ventures like Peter Cook's The Establishment club and the new satirical magazine *Private Eye*, a market was emerging for everyday comic resistance (Carpenter, 2000).

Importantly, the explosion of interest in satire meant that comic writers and performers had to adapt quickly to new mediums – whereas *Beyond the Fringe* had been a stage show, *TW3*, *I'm Sorry I'll Read That Again* and *Private Eye* embraced different media; TV, Radio and print journalism. Many of the protagonists emerged from Oxbridge, proving themselves in university reviews, or gaining opportunities when jobs (for the boys) 'came up'. Out of this chaotic, yet productive milieu, the BBC commissioned a combination of satirists from Oxford and Cambridge, whose ongoing failure to stick with one name for their programme, initially led someone in the upper echelons of BBC management to refer to them as a bit of "a flying circus" (see Wilmut, 1980: 195). The movement from stage to screen, to international fame changed the form of the satire. What was most apparent in pages of *Private Eye* and the broadcast sketches of *TW3* was that 'everything was a target'; the aim was not so much to articulate a clear political position, but rather to mock 'all' political positions and public figures (Wagg, 2002).

Rather than a progressive selling out of 'high ideals' or any supposedly left-wing values then, this period saw a more contingent and unfolding process of experimentation, where the form and the substance of comedy is at stake. Whereas *Beyond the Fringe* had used the power of satire to subvert serious issues of imperial decline, global security and the social justice implications of austerity, the *Monty Python* show concentrated the sillier side of the establishment through quick sketches, songs, and animation. Of course, silly jokes can be found in *Beyond the Fringe*, as in sketches about the relative utility of Wittgensteinian language philosophers 'going to the shop', or – as will be discussed in section 3 – the valorization of the 'working classes' as stoic, tea drinking, deferential gardeners in the 'Aftermyth of War'. However, I would argue that the fast-moving form of *Monty Python* augmented the satirical thrust somewhat.[2] The satire of the upper classes that emerged was less subtle, *more of a celebration.*

In the 'Upper Class Twit of the Year' sketch, competitors are described by a sports commentator, noting that conditions were "firm under foot" as the twits gallop out onto the field for a "splendid afternoon's sport".[3] These "prize idiots" number "Vivian Smith-Smythe-Smith; he's in the grenadier guards, but he can count up to four!"; "Simon Zinc Trumpet Harris; he's an old Etonian and married to a very attractive

---

[2] As the defining histories of this period recount (Wilmut, Carpenter), aspects of this augmentation can be understood through tracing the career paths of comedians like John Cleese, who worked on the radio series *I'm Sorry I'll Read That Again*. To compare, the high-brow, theatre-based satire of *Beyond the Fringe*, was a far cry from the fast paced, pun heavy, radio sketch show that was marketed to children and young people. Indeed, by way of illustration, it was this combination of Cleese with Tim Brooke Taylor, Bill Oddie and Graeme Garden, who would go on to form *The Goodies*, that saw the first outing for the comedy song 'Stuff that Gibbon', which became a chart success for the Goodies with 'Funky Gibbon'.

[3] Monty Python, 'Upper Class Twit of the Year', 4 January 1970, https://www.youtube.com/watch?v=zGxSM5y7Pfs (accessed 4 May 2020).

table lamp"; "Nigel Incubator Jones, his best friend is a tree and in his spare time he's a stockbroker"; "Gervais Brooke-Hamster, he's in the wine trade and his father uses him as a waste paper basket"; and "Oliver St John-Mollusc, another old Etonian, his father was cabinet minister and his mother won the Derby".[4]

The horse-like twits engage in a series of heats to find the *outstanding twit*. It's a struggle because they initially face the wrong way, and don't understand the concept of a starter's gun. When it gets going, they face a range of testing challenges: walking in a straight line without falling over ("Oliver's worst event"); the matchbox jump (Vivian refuses the jump), kicking the beggar ("the beggar is down, oh the crowd really love that"). Eventually, the competitors are completely spread out across the field. Oliver can't get over the match box: "he's magnificent this man, he doesn't know when he's beaten, he doesn't know when he's winning either, he has no sort of sensory apparatus known to man". They struggle to shoot the rabbit, which is tied to the spot, Oliver is dead because he's run himself over; and they struggle to "take the bras off the debutantes from the back", before the final event where they have to shoot themselves. Gervais wins and his coffin receives a gold medal.[5]

How is the evisceration possible? What happened to the careful and pointed subversion of class and rank? On one level, the refiguring of the upper classes as figures of fun, a set of grotesque buffoons to laugh at, and indeed to cheer their eventual demise, could be seen as a success; the gradual opening up of a social repression that had characterized post-war Britain. Indeed, the confidence and professional skills that the Monty Python team gained from their success meant they could go on to explore other forms of social repression, like religion in *Life of Brian*, via the longer and more sophisticated format of a feature film. On another level, however, the reduction of satire to a mediatized form, an easy joke that we can all get and cheer along, raises questions about the politics of everyday comic resistance. While *Beyond the Fringe* played in theatres, where the nuance and edge of the satire could be explored in intimate detail, in fact where Harold Macmillan even went to see Cook's impersonation, the later satires were mediated by radio and TV. One effect of this mediation was to perform politics (and wider society) in a very particular way.

---

[4] Ibid.

[5] Ibid.

Stephen Wagg (1992) argues that the popular form of satire brings together two apparently separate spheres, the private and the public, and presents itself as an important way to both understand *and survive* their clash. The fact that politicians, or the establishment, were *a target* of these satires is a sign that the 'public world' was to be regarded with caution: as invasive of the private sphere of individual freedom. On this view, an accelerated, indeed, *hyper satirical* form in *Monty Python* can be thought of as part of a more generalized turning away from public politics associated with liberal capitalism. What began, as an open, messy, chaotic process of 'learning how to do' satire had become a commodified performance, where the audience, the medium and the satirical subject were rehearsing a set of critical oppositions that had become their own end.

2 Ambiguities of the satire boom

From the generalization of an anti-establishment perspective, which allowed a wider audience to question the arrogance of empire and the privilege of elites, to the overriding focus on the absurdity of British life, the satire boom foregrounded an ironic reflexivity. However, this section will argue that we should also reckon with the contingencies of satirical success; the ethical ambiguities and limits that are (re)produced in comic resistance. Who is able to speak satire? What are they able to say? In this way, I will argue, the satire boom can be associated with the legitimation of a particular model of satirical agency 'as' white, masculine, upper-class, English and so on. Against the self-congratulatory myth of British satire – as a critical outpouring of self-deprecation and irony – the class, racial and gendered dimensions of certain routines and jokes suggest a rather more problematic achievement.

Aspects of this critique of satire draw from the instrumental approach. On this view, the primary question was impact: did satirical resistance *really* change anything? Interestingly, this was a dilemma that the satirists felt themselves, often struggling with the high expectations carried in the name of 'satire'. Instead, their overriding commitment was to comedy. Just as Peter Cook actually held Macmillan in high regard, he also encouraged humour about 'all' political sides, sometimes admonishing audience members at his Establishment club who complained about jokes that targeted liberal movements like CND (campaign for Nuclear Disarmament) (Wagg, 2002). Indeed, this 'joking about all sides' was a common motif, designed to nurture the amiable and clever style of satire; quick witted, not unkind. As Jonathan Miller recounted: "None of us approached the world with a satirical indignation.... We had no reason to – we were all very comfortably off, and doing very nicely.... Peter and I came from professional middle-class families anyway, and had nothing to complain of" (see Wilmut, 1980: 17). Indeed, not only were the comedians of the satire boom overwhelmingly male, middle-class, privately educated products of Oxbridge, they also took to the *business of comedy* with ease. As Wagg (2002: 322) recounts of the entrepreneur in the group, David Frost:

> Frost, a Cambridge contemporary of Cook, was the principal means by which 'satirical' comedy was brought before a mass audience and, thus, into British popular culture. Frost has never known a working life outside of television. Even as an undergraduate at Cambridge University (1958–61) he was working intermittently for Anglia Television, procuring comedy material (usually written by Cook) and interviewing local people. His apparent interest has always been in the medium itself and in techniques of presentation. [...] Frost ... was probably the first to see the possibilities of 'satire' as a new, effectively populist discourse.

As the previous section suggested, the success of satire in popular culture, also raised a set of critical questions. With the movement from stage, to radio, from TV programs to films and – in the case of John Cleese – advertising, it became possible to view the culmination of the 'satire boom' as a progressive process of commodification.

Beyond such instrumental and critical concerns, however, the selection of personnel and the substance of the humour can further problematize the ethics of satirical resistance. On this view, it is not simply an 'accident' that the central protagonists are male, upper-class, privately educated and so on. Instead, we must ask about how such everyday hierarchies of social difference are part of the performative politics of comic resistance. Histories of this period recount how the formation of satire clubs in the colleges of Oxford and Cambridge was a fundamentally gendered affair. Performances were rehearsed and tried out in 'Smokers': all-male events where you could smoke, and where acts could try out more offensive material. As Roger Wilmut (1980: 1) recounts, the first 80 years of Footlights were almost exclusively male:

> Since membership of the club was limited to men, female impersonation was a necessary performing art until 1932

when 'real women' were included in the cast for the first time. The result was felt to be such an unmitigated disaster that the following year's show was called *No More Women* and it was not until the early 1960s that female membership of the actual club was allowed ...

As well as blanket exclusion, there were converse patterns of male inclusion. As the satire boom kicked off, it really was a question of finding the 'right chaps' to do the job. Indeed, when women were included in shows in like *I'm Sorry I'll Read That Again* or *TW3*, it was usually as 'the woman'; a character actor, who also sang. This speaks to a longer tradition in comedy of *including women* in certain ways: as the butt of a joke, either as stereotype 'wife' or 'mother', or in overtly sexualized terms, as object of affection, or 'tart' (Andrews, 1998). In one variation, *The Frost Report* included a stock character 'ditzy woman', a kind of pretty girl who would link between sketches, all the while imagining (wrongly) that this was in fact her show. Further, to recall the 'Upper Class Twits' sketch, the twits are all men until they get to the event where they have to take the debutantes' bras off. Indeed, Stephen Wagg (1992: 270) identifies this with deeper problematic:

> A strong strain of cruelty runs through Monty Python and much of it is located in the female characters ... a woman contestant in a TV quiz programme, who doesn't like 'darkies', wins a blow on the head; another middle-aged woman, accompanied by her friend 'Mrs N[*****]baiter', treats her son like a recalcitrant child even though he is, apparently, the Minister for Overseas Development; knitting ladies guard a nuclear submarine; a Somerset landlady applies lard to her cat's boil, oblivious to Hitler and Himmler, wearing a full Nazi regalia, plotting in her dining room to take Stalingrad; members of the Batley Townswomen's Guild re-enact the Battle of Pearl Harbour.... Women were thus often portrayed as reactionary and repressive creatures, holding screeching dominion over the domestic sphere.

This raises an important question about the capacity of resistance to reproduce the very things it seeks to oppose. By turning against power, especially imperial arrogance and the racist world-view it manifests, satire often needed to find a way to represent such power in order to subvert it. While the intention is clearly to *oppose* racist and fascist politics through ridicule, it is arguable that imputing those ideas to women is merely a displacement of the violence; indeed, one which fits with a peculiarly male world-view that can equate the violence of empire with the social authority of mothers.

This creates two ethical limits for thinking about comic resistance. First, an apparent anger at imperial racism is displaced onto women (indeed without challenging the circulation of racist tropes itself). In one interview, Eric Idle backed this up by saying Python "mocks all the authority figures. Including mothers. Especially mothers" (BBC 1, *Omnibus* 5 October 1990). Second, more profoundly, it seeks to bluntly dismiss and vilify racism and imperialism, rather than to unpick and foreground the ongoing practices that make such rationalities possible. To underline, I don't think this use of the 'N-word' can or should be understood in terms of a lazy 'it was a different time' type argument. The point is that Monty Python are trying to use it critically – indeed, in the sketch, the woman eventually blows up, frustrated at the thought of the Minister for Overseas Development addressing the Commons on the subject of Rhodesia. In response, the surviving characters suggest that it is probably a good thing that she died. However, in using the term critically they also efface the difficult elements of imperialism; of how racism and gender politics both emerge from and produce a vision of Britain that has 'progressed' from its previous and regrettable violence(s).

Stuart Ward argues that such ambiguities can be understood more clearly if we situate them in terms of the experience and personal ambivalence(s) felt in relation to imperial decline. On this view, the class, gender and racial privileges of the satire boom are neither accidental, nor *precisely* the critical point to focus on. Rather, he argues that 'much of the apparently progressive criticism of the British establishment that characterized the satire boom was in fact fundamentally rooted in a *nostalgic* reflection on the imperial past' (Ward, 2001b: 92, emphasis added.). Indeed, such an argument probably helps to reconcile the curious mix of 'amiable' caricatures of the establishment that went alongside occasionally cruel stereotypes of social conservatism. As Ward (2001b: 92) maintains: 'While on the face of it the satire boom had the character of a good-humoured acknowledgement of new post-imperial realities, closer examination reveals an underlying resentment towards those who had promised a more grandiose role for Britain in the post-war world.' On the one hand, he cites the sexism of *Private Eye* in its coverage of the Profumo affair as an example of the resentful glee with which this new form of anti-establishment satire could take a political scandal and magnify its entertainment value through titillation and ridicule. On the other hand, he argues that the satire boom exhibited a fundamental disconnect between the lampooning of imperial values and the portrayal of anti-colonial movements themselves.

In 'Black Equals White', for example, Peter Cook interviews the leader of the 'Pan African Federal Party', Mr Akiboto Nobitsu (played with an exaggerated accent by Jonathan Miller), in order to address colonial arrogance, changing hierarchies and so on. Although, as Ward (2001b: 103–5) argues, this did not imply any 'sympathy' for the cause of colonial nationalism:

Nobitsu: There can be no progress, Mr Edwards, until you Englishmen stop looking down your noses at us Africans.

Edwards: [looking down his nose] Yes I think I see what you mean …
[…]

Edwards: Mr Nobitsu, how do you view the imprisonment of your colleague, Mr Bandabaku?

Nobitsu: The imprisonment of Mr Bandabaku is a most immoral, disgusting and illegal act and definitely not cricket. It is an outrageous and despicable act, and I am in favour of it as it lets me get on with a little bit of agitating of my own.

Edwards: Mr Nobitsu, do you in any way condone the violent methods used by your party to further their ends?

Nobitsu: By 'violent methods', Mr Edwards, I presume you are referring to the isolated and sporadic outbreaks of entire communities being wiped out?

Edwards: Yes, I did have that in mind.

Such sketches demonstrate a general scepticism towards the integrity of nationalist struggles. As per the marginalization of women, this was a period where African and South Asian characters were played by white actors; whether 'blacking up' for stage or screen, or by affecting a stereotypical and exaggerated accent *pace* Miller's Nobitsu.[6] At best, this suggests a lack of interest in the wider politics of imperialism and

---

[6] Another example was John Bird's impersonation of Kenyatta who, with exaggerated accent, envisaged an attack on England with poison spears and the expectation that he would 'assume the office of the Queen'.

its legacies. At worst, it confirms the image of the 'satire boom' as a reinvention of imperial rationalities through a period of instability and decline. Citing Kenneth Tynan's view of the new breed of satirists as 'anti-reactionary without being progressive', Ward (2001b: 109) describes the mood of satire as: 'a striking manifestation of the deep sense of ambivalence that permeated British culture in the age of imperial decline – evincing at one and the same time an overweening pride, self-deprecatory shame, and a feeling of powerlessness to embrace a post-imperial future.' On this view, the comic resistance of satire enacts a vernacular language of global politics that contains critical possibilities and ethico-political limits; a paradoxical combination of anti-establishment irony and resentment of 'whatever' provoked its emergence in the first place.

3 Irony: a new language of global politics

Despite the ethical ambiguities that pervade sketches in *Monty Python* and *Beyond the Fringe*, this section will argue that we should read the satire boom as productive. Far from diminishing the performative significance of comic resistance, the generalization of satire through mediatized and commodified forms suggests something quite significant about the changes in global market life that Britain was experiencing. If elements of this discourse reproduced colonial and reactionary logics by displacing them onto classed, raced and gendered subjects then this provides important insight about 'what is stake' in everyday resistance. The market form of irony that emerged through the satire boom left behind a critical public discourse capable of reflecting its own ambiguities. At the time, this was evident through widespread public and private critiques of satire for 'selling out'. The next chapter will look at how 'alternative comedy' targeted the 'Oxbridge mafia', in the process developing a range of more political *and politicized* routines.

My central argument is that there is a critical reflexivity in British comedy, which can – but does not necessarily – encourage a form of humour that yields a perspective on contingency. Once this language is generalized through the commodity form, indeed via the relentless expansion of mediatized society, it is not really a question of whether this or that sketch embodies the 'correct' ethics or resistant politics. While an important critical reflex, the isolation of particular sketches can downplay the circulation and re-performance of comic resistance. Both the 'instrumental' critique that satire and had 'sold out' and the more sophisticated 'critical' position that satire emerged from – *and largely reproduced* – the ambivalences of post-imperial decline, therefore miss the performative politics of agency and satirical form. There is a politics of emergence; comedy becomes an important cultural genre through which British political discourse comes to know itself. As such, the capacity of comedians to reflect upon their work, change it, or – as is common – *criticize each other*, can be thought of as an everyday politics of globalization.

After the 'satire boom', comedy was no longer 'just a laugh' or an idle whimsy, but had become part of the reflexive discourse of politics. Paradoxically, of course, the (gleeful) subversion of empire and the establishment performed a new phase of upper-class, university educated, 'boldness-to-reflect'. Yet, in performative terms, it also established and disseminated a new vernacular through which political discourse about global market life could continue. Doubt, self-deprecation, suspicion of pomposity and self-interest, had become key tenets of public critical thought that would come to inform not only comedy but also such disparate pursuits as journalism and punk. Reflexively, the satirical market subject is always-already aware of its limits; just as Peter Cook had famously modelled his Establishment club on all those Berlin satirical nightclubs that 'did so much to stop the rise of Hitler', satire could – at its best – reflect the wider limits of post-imperial Britain. Here, I will argue, an understated technique can be found in the juxtaposition of imperial decline with the everyday, utterly mundane position of the working classes. In this way, satire reflected not simply the pomposity of the upper classes, with all the associated and parochial limits of resentment identified by Ward, but, as well, the relational politics of class within the national and global market discourse.

Everyday class politics

An important but sometimes neglected element of the satirical turn against the upper classes was the far more nuanced and open-ended consideration of class *relations*. In particular, the place of working-class men, how they inhabit and 'endure' the structural inequalities of post-imperial Britain, licensed a consideration of the cultural bases of global market life, inviting reflection on the caricatures of stoic deference that prevailed. Quintessentially, the 'Aftermyth of War' develops a prescient subversion of popular discourses of 'plucky Englanders' pulling together to beat 'Jerry'. Telling the story of the war through the experiences of people from different class positions, they pose a critical question as to the authenticity of national myths:

Bennett [A middle-class lady]:	I will always remember that weekend war broke out. I was at a house party at Clifton with the Asters. We sat around … we sat around listening to the moving broadcast by Mr Churchill, or Mr Chamberlain as he then was. […] But I did not feel then, that all was quite lost. Immediately afterwards I got on the telephone to Berlin to try and have a word with Herr Hitler, who'd been so awfully kind to us on our last visit to Germany that summer. Unfortunately, the line was engaged, there was nothing I could do to avert the carnage of the next six years.
Moore:	Mr Charles Spedding of Hoxton remembers …
Cook [A working-class man]:	I'll always remember that day that war was declared, I was out in the garden at the time, planting out some chrysants. It was a grand year for chrysants 1939, I wish we could have another one like it. My wife come out to me in the garden and told me, the ghastly news about the outbreak of hostilities. Never mind my dear, I said to her, you put on the kettle, we'll have a nice cup of tea.
Air Raid Warden:	Put out that light [air raids sirens]
Moore [A middle-class man]:	All over Britain the humble little people showed the same spirit of courage.
Miller [Working-class man]:	You could always tell the difference between theirs and ours. Ours had a sort of steady reliable British hum, rather like a holy old bumble bee. Theirs on the other hand had a sort of horrible vicious intermittent whine like a ghastly foreign mosquito.[7]

---

[7] Again, this could be read as a satire of reactionary attitudes in the military, indeed Ward notes the Cockney accent of the private, suggesting displacement onto the working class. Or else, the comedy creates a liminal figure, a regrettable relic maybe, whose politics are repugnant, yet whose accent and bloody-minded confidence might 'have tickled a nostalgic nerve in that same audience'.

Beyond the Fringe, 'The Aftermyth of War', Part 1, date unknown, https://www.youtube.com/watch?v=ZZaBbH4bCjY (accessed 4 May 2020).

This long sketch is often recalled through its funniest scene, where an upper-class officer played by Cook, tells another junior officer: "Perkins I want you to lay down your life, we need a futile gesture at this stage, it'll raise the whole tone of the war. Get up in a crate Perkins, pop over to Bremen, take a shufti, don't come back." Much like the 'Upper Class Twits', the scene points to the wretched nature of the upper classes and their cavalier attitude to war. "Goodbye Perkins, God I wish I was going too", Perkins: "Goodbye Sir, or is it Au-Revoir?" It concludes starkly: "No, Perkins."[8] However, the real substance of the sketch is to set up different classes *as united* in the war effort:

Cook:	From the rugby fields into the air.
Miller:	From the squash courts into the clouds.
Bennett:	From the skips into the spitfires.
Miller:	This was war.
Bennett [Middle-class officer with pipe]:	I had a pretty quiet war really, I was 'one of the few', we were stationed down at Biggin Hill. One Sunday we, we got word Jerry was coming in, over Hastings I think, I got up first because I could, and everything was very calm and peaceful. England lay like a green carpet below. The war seemed worlds away. I could see Tunbridge Wells, the sun glinting on the river, I remembered that last weekend I spent there with Celia, that summer of 39. Suddenly Jerry was coming at me out of a bank of cloud, I let him have it, and I, well I think I must have got him in the wing because he spiralled past me out of control [...] I always remember this, I caught a glimpse of his face, do you know, he smiled. Funny thing war.[9]

The tone plays with the post-war idea that victory meant something deeper about the 'values' of Britain, that there was a fundamental decency about 'the English', which could be located in their diversity.

---

8   *Beyond the Fringe*, 'The Aftermyth of War', Part 2, date unknown, https://www.youtube.com/watch?v=7R_l9KbYpag (accessed 4 May 2020).

9   *Beyond the Fringe*, 'The Aftermyth of War', Part 1.

The idiot upper classes, the humble officer class, and the good-natured 'underlings' who lived through the Blitz:

> Cook [working-class accent]: That was the night they got Pithy Street. I'll always remember it. I was out in the garden at the time, planting out some deadly Nightshade for the Bosch. My wife came out to me in the garden and told me the abominable news, thousands have died in Pithy Street, she said. Never you mind the thousands who've died, I said to her, you put on the kettle, we'll have a nice cup of tea.[10]

It goes on in this fashion; an officer tells a working-class soldier, "I'd never really known men of your class before. Let me say just this, it's been a privilege", they shake hands and go to fight. Cook's working-class character returns again, this time "planting out some carrots for the night fighters", to recall the time his wife told him about rationing: "Never mind my dear, I said to her, you put on the kettle, we'll have a nice cup of boiling hot water."[11]

Again, it would be possible to render this through the instrumental critique, that it doesn't change class relations because it simply laughs at them, or equally through the critical position that it expresses the class position of the satirists and their own 'self-deprecatory shame'. But this would miss the productive qualities of comedy, how returning to the joke, re-telling it, and augmenting the line can alter the nature of the resistance. In other sketches, Cook sharpened the edge of his satire to question the justice of how class affected opportunity. In 'Why I'd Rather Be a Judge than a Miner', he laments the fact that he could have been a judge, but he never had the Latin to pass the rigorous judging exams. Whereas the exams to be a miner involved just one question: "Who are you? I got 75% on that." And he questions the boredom and drudgery of mining: "this black substance is coal alright, jolly good the very thing we're looking for". While seemingly a sneer at the monotonous work of coalmining, the various versions of the sketch culminate in the same punchline that, in the case of mining, as soon as you're too old and sick and stupid to do the mining, you have to go, "whereas the very opposite applies with the judges".[12]

---

[10] *Beyond the Fringe*, 'The Aftermyth of War', Part 2.
[11] Ibid.
[12] *Beyond the Fringe*, 'Why I'd Rather Be a Judge than a Miner', date unknown, https://www.youtube.com/watch?v=ed0UgcXZCh8 (accessed 4 May 2020).

This perspective on class matured into a mainstay of the double act between Cook and Moore, or Pete'n'Dud, in their TV show *Not Only, But Also*, to present the everyday experiences and thoughts of working-class men as a fulcrum for reflecting on the ridiculousness and pomposity of everyday popular culture. As two blokes down the pub they recall the various difficulties they experience, getting into bed, reading the *Swiss Family Robinson* only to be startled by the phone "Do you know who it was? Bloody Betty Grable", wanting Pete to go and dance with him.[13] On another night, "tap tap tap on the window, do you know who it was? Bloody Greta Garbo". Dud replies to ever more fantastical stories with "Well it's funny you should say that, 'cos the other night ...". 'Funny' is repeated throughout the sketch to mean incongruous, but the repetition makes it funny, per se. It transpires that Dud has been visited in his bed by Jane Russell, a move which is too much for him. Both men turn down the amorous advances of these Hollywood actresses and decide to finish their night (and the sketch) by going to the cinema. These sketches are jokes about how empty life is, a basic cynicism to the everyday realities of the class system and, by extension working life. Yet they bring to the fore working-class characters, from an initial subversion of stoic deference, to a foregrounding of working-class men reflecting on hierarchies in the world around them.

Conclusion

In conclusion, this chapter has identified the potentialities and limits of the satire boom for imagining an everyday resistance to global politics. While the cultural politics of imperial decline elicited a number of important comic resistances that foregrounded the value of irony and self-deprecation in the national discourse on global politics, the success of the satire boom can be qualified by a number of post-imperial ambiguities, namely: commodification, mediatization, as well as manifold hierarchies of class, gender and race. While these ambiguities can support both instrumental critiques that the satirists 'sold out' and critical observations about the role of post-imperial anger/shame in re-legitimating a violent social order, my argument has sought to underline the contingent production and politics of this resistant vernacular. On the one hand, the satire boom was not useless in the task of questioning and resisting such ambiguities. In

---

[13] Peter Cook and Dudley Moore (In the pub), date unknown, https://www.youtube.com/watch?v=hvQq_tqB0jA (accessed 4 May 2020).

particular, by making class a locus of reflection and critique, satire was able to refigure the incisiveness and wit of the 'bon-mots' precisely to question everyday social hierarchies and privileges. Indeed, Stephen Wagg (1992: 269) conceives of this as a discourse that actually came to fruition in the work of Monty Python: 'The point about Python is that it represents a social critique and is not narrowly concerned with politics or politicians.' On the other hand, and while elements of this social critique were poorly figured and carried certain ethical limits that were identified in section 2, I argued that the vernacular of comic resistance established in the satire boom could be a reflexive discourse. In part, this is a function of the competition and rivalries between comedians seeking to outdo each other, yet it is also a result of the progressive, if contingent, politicization of humour itself. As subsequent chapters will now begin to draw out, once established, this new, ironic language for engaging in global politics, could provide a fulcrum for the ongoing politicization of everyday life in global context.

3

Alternative Comedy and Resistance to 'Thatcher's Britain'

Introduction

The emergence of (what became known as) 'alternative comedy' is widely regarded as an important critical moment in the history of British comedy, where comedians began to break with the idea that their craft was 'just for laughs' (Giappone, 2017). A range of new acts fundamentally reinvented the nature and form of comedy to place in question prior conceptions of *the gag*, the audience, and the overall 'point' of humour. Whereas the satire boom had touched upon politics through the nature of its targets and a wider public debate over whether it really changed anything, alternative comedy foregrounded a set of *avowedly resistant* concerns with anti-racism, anti-sexism, anti-capitalism and 'Thatcher' (Lee, 2010; Schaffer, 2016).

While the previous chapter explored a certain 'anti-elitist elitism' in the satire boom, whose protagonists were mainly white, male, upper-class, Oxbridge and so on, the egalitarian politics of alternative comedy was often embodied in the comedians themselves, who came from 'art schools' and 'lesser universities'. Suddenly comedians were working-class, black, female, they had regional accents, were angry, or anarchic. A punk mentality informed their audience interactions as the new medium of 'stand-up' explored the possibilities of spontaneity, provocation and violence in humour (Sayle, 2016). In addition, surviving outside the Oxbridge production line of student reviews and BBC commissions required an alternative economic model. Their circuit consisted of pioneering new comedy clubs like *The Comedy Store* and the *Comic Strip*, as well as regional arts centres, student unions and pubs. Diverse backgrounds, alternative pathways and radical innovations in 'stand-up' would ultimately create a form of comedy that resembled an artistic or political movement (British Comedy Guide, 2016). Gone were the *bon mots* and witty reflections of satire, to reveal a more experimental, uncompromising and 'revolutionary' set of practices. Indeed, this more 'politicized' understanding began to inform the wider self-understanding of comedy. As Stewart Lee (2010: 2–3) recounts:

> there was a Year Zero attitude to 1979. Holy texts found in a skip out the back of the offices of the London listings magazine *Time Out* tell us how, with a few incendiary post-punk punchlines, Alexei Sayle, Arnold Brown, Dawn French, and Andy de la Tour destroyed the British comedy hegemony of upper-class Oxbridge Satirical Songs and Working-Class Bow Tie-Sporting Racism. Then with the fragments of these smashed idols and their own bare hands, they built the pioneering stand-up clubs *The Comedy Store* and the *Comic Strip*. In so doing they founded the egalitarian Polytechnic of Laughs that is today's comedy establishment. Every religion needs a genesis myth, and this is contemporary British stand-up comedy's very own creation story. (Lee, 2010: 2–3)

Situating alternative comedy as an everyday practice of resistance in global context raises important questions about 'what' is being resisted and 'why'? On the one hand, the self-identity of alternative comedy was forged against upper-class satirists like John Cleese who were regarded as 'established' or 'untouchable' in the industry. While alternative comedians would occasionally mix with them during benefit gigs like Amnesty's *Secret Policeman's Ball*, the tendency was to treat them as antiquated, apolitical and posh. On the other hand, a more virulent sense of opposition was felt towards the working-class comics who dominated light entertainment in the 1970s and 1980s (Sutton, forthcoming). Comics like Bernard Manning, Mike Reid and Jim Davidson were criticized for being racist, sexist and *above all* clichéd gag merchants. Although, such frictions might be regarded as 'merely professional', about rival personalities and egos in a superficial media profession, I will argue that there is more at stake.

By refusing the twin apologias of upper-class irony and working-class reactionary humour, alternative comedy allowed for a moment of critical insight on the everyday experience of globalization. Alternative comedy provided an important reflective discourse that emphasized the cultural political economy of market life, how irony could not absolve the upper classes of their deep post-imperial ambiguities, and how racism and sexism in working-men's club comedy were symptomatic of a defensive, nativist discourse on liberalization and globalization. Through shows like *The Young Ones* and *Alexei Sayle's Stuff*, alternative comedy would prick at the universalist pomposity of neoliberalism and Thatcherite denials of society by exposing the everyday work of prejudice in legitimating privatization, deregulation, and de-industrialization.

This argument is developed over three sections. Section 1 identifies the broadening of social and ethical concerns in 'alternative comedy' that saw a more avowed association with the left. Section 2 engages a central dilemma between the 'success' of alternative comedy in promoting certain values in the mainstream of UK political culture, such as equality, political correctness, and the obvious potential for recuperation as the critical edge was superseded by TV-friendly irony. These tensions are explored via the work and personal reflections of Alexei Sayle, someone who was both formative in the success of alternative comedy and critical of its 'selling out'. Against the myth of alternative comedy as progressive (which is easily subject to instrumental and critical qualifications), my analysis suggests a dynamic and conflictual reckoning with the tensions of global market life. While a more critical concern with the ethics and politics of race, gender and sexuality were clearly a part of the story of alternative comedy, a focus on Alexei Sayle can help in questioning how such progressive values played a broader social role in the legitimation of global market rationalities (Brassett, 2018a).

In short, British comedy began to license a reflexive critique of its own close association with the very object of its material: the (British) state form of global capitalism. Indeed, this intensely self-critical tone would lay the comic groundwork for the emergence of a highly sophisticated form of irony that will be analysed in the next chapter. While Sayle identified the problematic relationship between alternative comedy and the British state form of global capitalism, many others embraced the successful mainstreaming of their careers. Section 3 therefore reflects on some of the unintended consequences of this new vision of comic resistance, by asking what possibilities and limits were instantiated.

On the one hand, the promotion of female and black comedians in the mainstream of British popular culture has important social and political consequences that should not be underestimated. Equally, alternative comedians would regularly do 'benefit gigs' for trade unions and the Labour Party, or, if they mixed with the Oxbridge set, Amnesty International. The birth of Comic Relief showed how such 'comic activism' could have a direct effect on global politics, educating a mass audience about international poverty and promoting humanitarian responsibility. On the other hand, however, this turn to embrace a market-friendly form of global humanitarianism performed a new set of critical limits within the vernacular. The emerging nexus between alternative comedy and celebrity politics caught the attention of an increasingly media-literate political class. With the demand for 'relatable' politicians and 'pan-demographic' political messages, party spin doctors began to seek out comedians to work as consultants or scriptwriters (Wagg, 2002). Thus, the relationship between comedy and politics moved from being one of straight opposition through satirical critique (which succeeded or failed), to usher in a more symbiotic relationship, where the mediatized spectacle of politics increasingly courted legitimacy via the *authenticity* of comedy.

1 The *right on* politics of alternative comedy

As the Introduction to this chapter suggested, the rise of (what came to be known as) alternative comedy is bound up in retrospective social myths that might over-determine its qualities and characteristics. Semantically, there is a good suggestion that the word *alternative* came from a project called 'Alternative Cabaret', which was set up by Tony Allen and Alexei Sayle (Giappone, 2017), but the wider and complex list of acts, routines and subjects implies that there was something more at stake in terms of identity and political values. Alternative comedy distinguished itself in opposition to mainstream British comedy, including both satire and the reactionary humour of stand-up comics like Bernard Manning. As Alexei Sayle noted: 'The whole point of what we were doing was surely to challenge the smug hegemony of the Oxford, Cambridge, public-schoolboy comedy network, as well as destroying the old-school working-men's club racists' (Sayle, 2013). This opposition to the work and social mores of existing comedians is a palpable element in the emergence of an everyday vernacular of comic resistance. Whereas the satire boom was forged against the imperial hubris of a declining order, alternative comedy was forged (in part) against the imperial hubris of a 'comedy establishment' that had somehow tranquillized the politics of decline. As Stewart Lee (2010: 3–4) recounts, this was partly an instrumental critique of the comfortable lives of satirists as they recycled their comedy format:

the slowly dissipating after-fart of the fifties and sixties satire boom meant that posh kids still helmed the high-profile left-field TV and radio shows, such as *Not the Nine O'Clock News* or *Radio Active*, as they do again today, and got to tour the Cambridge Footlights show to mid-range theatre venues in the south of England every year, still dressed in matching outfits and singing songs about the news at the piano.

However, the substance of the second attack on the 'old-school working-men's club racists', channelled a more critical concern with egalitarian politics that would fundamentally affect the wider perception of alternative comedy as *specifically left-wing*.

The political intensity of this movement is well illustrated by Alexei Sayle (2007), writing an Op Ed about Bernard Manning on the occasion of his death. Sayle described Manning as a nasty, unkind man. He conceded that he and some of his ilk may have been good comedians, practitioners of the craft, but they were mean and cynical:

> To placate whatever frazzled part of their mind acts as a conscience, Manning and his kind always draw some arbitrary line that they swear they won't cross, like an alcoholic telling himself that his drinking is under control as long as he stays off the barley wine. I seem to remember Bernard stating that though he might use [racist terms] in his act, he would never, ever tell a joke about 'disabled kiddies'. You could hear the self-regarding tremor in his voice as he said this, as if he was reluctantly admitting to being a humanitarian of similar stature to Nelson Mandela, Noam Chomsky or Aung San Suu Kyi. He always denied being a racist, claiming that he made fun of everybody, equally – 'politicians, bald-headed people, people with glasses on, the lot. I have a go at everybody and that's what makes everybody roar with laughter.' I notice he left [racist terms] out of his list, though. Those were the words people objected to him using; I can't remember much of a furore about his specky four-eyed barbs.

Working-men's club comics were regarded as 'backward' and reactionary in their humour, generally more comfortable doing jokes about 'Pakistanis, poofs and their wives' mothers' (Lee, 2010: 3). Indeed, this was something that alternative comedy sought to directly contest.

Upon opening the *Comedy Store*, Peter Rosengrad told the press that in terms of censorship 'anything goes' as long as 'it isn't racist or sexist'; while Ben Elton would commonly 'get the audience to boo people off' who tried any racist or sexist material (Schaffer, 2016: 379). For some comedians, this critical opposition towards reactionary humour was a substantive focus of 'the material', a point exquisitely captured in Tony Allen's parody: 'This drunk homosexual Pakistani squatter trade unionist takes my mother-in-law to an Irish restaurant. Says to the West Indian waiter, "Waiter, waiter, there's a racial stereotype in my soup"' (see Giappone, 2017: 395).

Drawing these points together, the radical political thrust of alternative comedy was consolidated in (the now famous) opposition to 'Thatcher'. This was a period in which being opposed to the Tory government under Thatcher became a common feature in comedy routines. Whether this was a coherent or committed ideological position is widely questioned. Indeed, as Jeremy Hardy (2017) recounted: 'There's this myth that all you had to do was say something rude about Mrs Thatcher and the whole audience would fall about, and you'd get massive laughs. You got no laughs, *you got funding*, but you got no laughs.'[1] However, regardless of the veracity of the myth, the combination of being anti-Oxbridge, anti-racist, anti-sexist, as well as orchestrating jokes and sketches around the Tory government, would have the effect of associating alternative comedy with a form of committed *left-wing* politics in the public consciousness (Schaffer, 2016).

A range of young comedians from across social classes, from different regions and ethnic backgrounds, developed a form of comedy that directly questioned British social attitudes (Lee, 2010; Brassett, 2016). In terms of performance, a key driver in this re-phrasing of British comedy was the new inspiration of 'stand-up', which provided a more

---

[1]   Jeremy Hardy (2017) critically reflects:

> 'the great myth is it was all very political and of course it really, really wasn't. People talked about politics in a slightly knowing way, but most of it was actually taking the piss out of the left, people like Alexei, who was raised as a Marxist-Leninist, and people like Tony Allen who was an anarchist, who was a you know a ranter at Hyde Park Corner, lots of knowing jokes about the politics of London. [...] by the time I started, it was jugglers, there was a bloke called ... Bernie Bennet who did a high wire act on a stage ... there were poets, there were people doing musical comedy, there were people with serious mental health issues, and there would be people who make ice sculptures, and all sorts of stuff.'

dynamic, but equally more aggressive, artistic and free-form version of humour (Cook, 2001). For example, Sayle (2014) recounted how Keith Allen would regularly finish routines by either throwing darts into the audience, stripping naked, or both. Crucially, this more confrontational aesthetic was not lost in the translation to TV.

The Young Ones was an ambitious reinterpretation of the sitcom, which saw four students share a rented house. Ostensibly a satire of student life, its characters included Vyvyan Basterd, or Vyv, a punk medical student who crashes through walls, puts a bomb on the doorbell to "pep it up a bit", and who enjoys taunting and beating Rik for being a virgin ("I am not a virgin!"). Rik is a committed political student, an anarchist poet, who is obsessed with Cliff Richard and sees fascism everywhere: "Neil, are these lentils South African? You bastard! You complete and utter bastard! Why don't you just go out and become a policeman? There's no difference you know [...] I suppose you hate gay people too, Hippy!"[2] Neil is constantly depressed, unable to keep up with the pace of events in the house. Dysfunctional and pathetic, he tries to commit suicide, but gets it wrong (Vyv: "I thought you were dead?" Neil: "Well that's no reason to hassle me on the toilet!"); everything to Neil is "heavy" or "bad Karma (again!)".[3] Finally, Mike is the 'straight man' in the group, essentially an old-style spiv, who presents as worldly and always has a money-making scheme (at one point he strikes oil in the basement and retains Vyvyan as his new private military).

Despite the deference to traditional set up and characterization, *The Young Ones* used the sitcom format to highlight the live energy and comic talent of the protagonists, often exploring connections between youth culture and everyday social issues. As well as the numerous comedians who appeared in the show, each episode managed to weave a live band performance into the narrative. This experimentalist attitude saw Vyv's hamster, Special Patrol Group (SPG) brought to life as a hard-nosed enforcer with a Scottish accent; or waste vegetables in the washing up bowl, who fell in love ice-skating on a dirty plate. At one point, Rik is overjoyed because: "finally after years of stagnation, the TV people have woken up to the need for locally based minority programmes ... made by amateurs, of interest to only two or three people, it's important right, it's now, and I want to watch."[4] In another

---

[2] *The Young Ones*, Series One, episode 1, 'Demolition', 9 November 1982, https://www.dailymotion.com/video/x57xoyp (accessed 6 May 2020).
[3] Ibid.
[4] Ibid.

scene, Alexei Sayle, who plays a different character every episode, is able to channel his live act; as the (apparently) Russian landlord, breaking the fourth wall to address the studio audience:

> 'I'm not really foreign, you know, I just do it to appear more sophisticated, [increasingly shouting in thick scouse accent] I mean nobody would buy Evian water if it was called Blackburn water, would they! Nobody'd wear Kicker boots if they were made in Scunthorpe. ABBA ABBA, Swedish!?! I knew them when they were a Lancashire clog dancing trio [...] Solzhenitsyn, Solzhenitsyn, a former pipe fitter welder from Harrogate!'

In addition to Sayle's critical reflections on the 'exotic international' in advertising, there is a recurrent focus on racism, from Rik's identification of fascism everywhere (re: the cost of the lentils: "I'm not paying you money to eat black men, I could become a pig and do that for free"),[5] to an exaggeratedly racist policeman.[6] More politically, in the episode entitled 'Cash', Vyv thinks he is pregnant (he is actually constipated); while worried about the impending 'baby' and how to raise it, Rik warns how hard it will be: "We can't, we haven't got any money. Vyvyan's baby will be a pauper. Oliver Twist, Geoffrey Dickens. Back to Victorian values. I hope you're satisfied, Thatcher!"[7] In this way, Rik articulates the wider thematic of anti-Tory politics that informs the dominant understanding of alternative comedy. Quintessentially, as the Young Ones inevitably finish university and contemplate their dismal options, Rik laments:

---

[5]   Ibid.

[6]   The policeman is so racist apparently, that he even mistakes a white man for a black man, perhaps because he is wearing dark gloves (the policeman also has sunglasses on). While his use of racist terms might appear in similar poor taste to some of the work in *Beyond the Fringe* and *Monty Python* considered in Chapter 2, it is now far clearer that the racism is being critiqued, that it is associated with fascism through ideas of 'totalitarian vegetables' or repeated references to fascist police.

[7]   *The Young Ones*, Series Two, episode 2, 'Cash', 15 May 1982, https://www.youtube.com/watch?v=2daYwNgyd3I As well as being a decent pun, which plays between Charles Dickens and the tory MP Geoffrey Dickens, the line is a direct reference to Thatcher's identification with and celebration of 'Victorian values'.

Rik: Thatcher's Britain! Thatcher's BLOODY Britain! Look at
        me. I'm young, I'm pretty. I've got 5 O Levels. Bloomin'
        good grades as well, considering I didn't do a sod of work
        cause I'm so hard. And look at me now! Homeless, cold,
        and prostitute.
Mike: Destitute Rik.
Rik: Oh glory be and save us Mike, do we have to mince with
        words? Anyway, so what? I can sell my body for a few good
        times if I want, what the hell, who cares? I'm gorgeous, I am
        sex. Women want me and they're prepared to pay. So don't
        you give me your phoney morality, its Dog-Eat-Cat in this
        world and you won't find me in a tin of Pedigree Chum.[8]

From alternative stand-up that mixed diverse acts and experimental
free-form audience interactions, to the ambitious and sometimes
absurdist reinvention of the sitcom that characterized *The Young
Ones*, alternative comedy appears to have retained a set of political
commitments to egalitarianism. There are obvious moments of critical
instability. Rik, for instance, is a satire 'of' a political student. In large
part, the joke is *on him*, and despite a few nice lines about Thatcher, his
character is a curious mix of 'critical anarchist' and 'good boy' from a
nice middle-class family, who ultimately embraces the neoliberal logic
of no alternative in this 'dog-eat-cat' world. As Jeremy Hardy (2017)
argued, a lot of alternative comedy 'was actually taking the piss out of
the left' and for all that *The Young Ones* reflected the new social changes
in British life, it sometimes steered close to the 'everything is a target'
feeling of the 'satire boom'. Despite such ambiguities, however, the next
section will argue that everyday comic resistance can be seen in more
productive terms. On this view, the ethical and political ambiguities
raised in alternative comedy – over racism, sexism, the 'proper' critique
of capitalism, the agency of the left and so on – can be understood as
part of an emerging political discussion about the cultural politics of
neoliberalism; part of an iterative processes of questioning and engaging
the everyday politics of global market life.

2 Alexei Sayle: resistance and recuperation

The politics of alternative comedy is bound up with a number of
ambiguities that underpin the instrumental and critical accounts of

---

[8]   Ibid., episode 6, 'Summer Holiday', 19 June 1984, https://www.youtube.com/
      watch?v=135hbzbI5tk (accessed 6 May 2020).

humour discussed in the Introduction and Chapter 1. On the one hand, it appears to miss its instrumental targets. Thatcher and the Tories won successive elections and managed to roll out some of the most far-ranging neoliberal reforms ever seen in the UK; deregulating labour, privatizing state utilities, liberalizing financial markets and so on. Indeed, a point that emerges from the literature is that shows like *Spitting Image* actually increased the popularity of Thatcher by making her seem 'fun' as her previously elite and anonymous cabinet became relatable (Wagg, 2002). In addition, the diverse social backgrounds and market innovations that drove a spirit of experimentation in alternative comedy were also very much 'of … [the] time'. As Schaffer (2016: 392) argues: 'Many pioneers of the alternative scene became successful businessmen with their own television companies, like Julian Clary and Jack Dee, while Ward's Comedy Store remains a global brand.' He cites the comedian Arthur Smith who observed: "What could be more Thatcherite than a stand-up comedian? Self-employed, un-unionized, unsupported by any namby-pamby arts grant, he has got on his bike and got a gig."

On the other hand, a more critical set of ambiguities can be identified in the relative social and cultural success of alternative comedy: what happens when resistant practices become mainstream? What began as a somewhat 'avant-garde' concern with anti-racism and anti-sexism was progressively generalized through acts like French and Saunders and Lenny Henry. From the 1980s onward, public sector broadcasters drove forward diversity and inclusion agendas that would fundamentally inform the wider legitimacy of neoliberal market relations of later decades. Indeed, Schaffer (2016: 394) argues that alternative comedy ultimately became another elitist discourse like satire: 'Frequently uninspired by the realities of working-class tastes and values, alternative comedians tended to offer a middle-class critique for middle-class audiences.'[9]

While sympathetic to these critiques, not least because they go to the heart of the claim that alternative comedy can be understood akin to a political movement of resistance, my approach will explore how such arguments *were themselves* anticipated in the work and personal reflections of certain comedians. Rather than fixing everyday comic resistance as a practice that 'does' or 'does not' work, or as a *pure form* of resistance that 'is' or 'is not' co-opted, this section will draw out the contingencies and subjectivities that are emergent *through*

---

[9]   Rather ironically, he further suggests: 'Despite their attacks on Oxbridge, most alternative comedians perpetuated an elitist approach to comedy, which only resonated with a small minority of people' (Schaffer, 2016: 396).

alternative comedy. In particular, I will read the everyday politics of alternative comedy through the prism of 'Alexei Sayle'. This can allow a productive engagement with the genuine dilemmas of being a political comedian at a time of rapid change in the state form of global capitalism (Gamble, 1994; Cerny, 1997). Despite certain limitations in their commodified product, alternative comedians like Sayle originated a form of comic resistance whose primary target was the cultural politics of globalization; how global rationalities and practices are promoted, enforced and contested in everyday social relations of race, gender and class. Running through his work is a critical commitment to de-naturalize the assumed universalisms of globalization that were popular in neoliberal government rhetoric; not least the idea that inequality was a 'natural' outcome of 'free' market competition. In *The Young Ones* episode entitled 'Bambi', when the housemates compete on University Challenge against 'Footlights College Oxbridge', Sayle, playing a train driver, performs a diatribe against the upper classes. While aspects of the piece are reminiscent of Cook's 'I'd Rather Have Been a Judge than a Coal Miner' discussed in the previous chapter, it typically makes a more aggressive cut:

> 'I never really wanted to be a train driver you know. I mean, they told me when I left school, if I got two CSEs, when I left school I'd be head of British Steel. That's a lot of nonsense, innit? I mean, you look at statistics, right. 83% of top British management have been to a public school and Oxbridge, right? 93% of the BBC have been to a public school and Oxbridge, right? 98% of the KGB have been to a public school and Oxbridge. All you get from a public school, right – one, you get a top job, right, and two, you get an interest in perverse sexual practices. I mean, that's why British management's so inefficient. As soon as they get in the boardroom, they're all shutting each other's dicks in the door! "Go on, give it another slam, Sir Michael!" BAM! OW OW OW! "Come on, Sir Geoffrey, let's play the Panzer commander and the milkmaid, EW EW EW EW! YOO HOO!"'

While this combination of class critique and absurd imagery echoes elements of the Upper Class Twits, the critical focus on market hierarchies is more acute. Against naturalized images of free market neoliberalism, Sayle puts the emphasis on how class – *and class privilege* – skews the system.

In subsequent reflections, he suggested that this class critique had a very personal slant because the 'Bambi' episode included several members of the 'Oxbridge mafia'. For Sayle (2013), this amounted to a betrayal of the resistant potential of alternative comedy: 'What I didn't understand, despite all my years of Marxist study groups, was that every revolution contains within it the seeds of its own destruction, and ours soon began to mutate in ways I could never have predicted.' He recalls turning up on the set of 'Bambi' to find several generations of the Cambridge Footlights crew and remonstrating with the writers: "I thought these people were the enemy!", only to receive the reply: "No, that was just you." "We never subscribed to your demented class-war ravings" (Sayle, 2013). In this way, Sayle's *own experience* can be read through the dilemma between resistance and recuperation:

> I realised that what had begun – in my mind – as a radical experiment was slowly moving towards the centre, and I had ceased to be its leader. Not that I should paint myself as some sort of exemplar, a Bill Hicks-like saint who held himself above the seductive lures of success. I craved the money, the big audiences and the fame that all the others craved: I just wanted to do it without getting my hands dirty by making what I thought of as compromises – or by being best friends with Stephen Fry. Also, it took me years to accept that not everybody wanted to spend a rare night out being shouted at by a rabid, opinionated, fat man. (Sayle, 2013)

Alexei Sayle's intimate struggles with the commodification of alternative comedy are an important illustration of the politics of resistance. For Sayle, alternative comedy was supposed to be a form *of radical* resistance. In particular, *Alexei Sayle's Stuff* would regularly feature satirical critiques of Tory agendas. In one episode, he parodied the demonization of social workers through the right-wing press, with Sayle's character violently questioning social workers about why they didn't do more to stop various historical tragedies such as Vlad the Impaler in Middle Ages Transylvania ("Why was it that throughout this horrific cataclysm of blood, Lambeth Social Services did nothing to stop it?"); of Herod's slaughter of the innocents ("Where was the Haringey childcare officer?" She replies: "Judea, in the year of our Lord, was technically outside my jurisdiction").[10] In such vignettes,

---

[10] *Alexei Sayle's Stuff*, Series One, episode 1, 13 October 1988, https://www.youtube.com/watch?v=8_VdpqQfSPI (accessed 6 May 2020).

Sayle articulated an everyday comic resistance to the cultural form of neoliberal globalization, actively de-naturalizing the affective slogans of neoliberal deregulation.

However, this articulation of a left-wing political critique of globalization was not some straightforward agenda that 'impacts' or not. Rather, it should be figured as a wider negotiation of resistant agency, indeed, part of an ongoing question about what the left is and what it stands for. In particular, Sayle's commitment to Marxism meant he doubted any turn to social democracy, instead articulating a more profound critique of the capitalist state under the Tories. The 'seeds of destruction' that he associated with alternative comedians who worked with the Oxbridge mafia, might also speak of a lost narrative of contest and critique within the British left, more broadly:

> 'one of the weird things about the left is their obsession with slogans, writing slogans on the wall, you know, slogans like "jobs not bombs", as if Mrs Thatcher's gonna be walking up Wigan high street [in high-pitched voice] "Oh jobs not bombs, oh ok!" For a start she wouldn't have a clue where Wigan was: Mrs Thatcher has special compasses made with the North taken off.
>
> 'I do a lot of left-wing benefits and one of the weird things about left-wing audiences is that you tell a joke and then there's a five second delay in which the joke is politically vetted and then they laugh. Like you say, Stalin was a bit of loony wasn't he, and they go [pretentious intellectual voice] "Stalin was a bit of a looney, hmm, yes I've got definite disagreements with Stalin's collectivisation of the gulags, yes, Hahahahaha." And they're really worried in case you say anything suspect, you know, like you say, these two women go into a shop right, and they go "Oh my god he's mentioned women, he's gonna say they're lesbians in a minute, we're gonna be laughing at lesbians, oh no! He's gonna say their black and we're gonna be laughing at black lesbians, oh my god oh my god no no no!" Honestly, that is not my style. Anyway, these two black lesbians go into a shop ...'[11]

---

[11] Alexei Sayle on Politics, October 1988, https://www.youtube.com/watch?v=vDAJQY5FMIw (accessed 29 March 2017).

This teasing out of tensions in left-wing politics is important for understanding the awkward fit between Sayle's form of comic resistance and the mythical narrative of ethical progress associated with alternative comedy. In his satires of the left, Sayle performs a clearly Marxist focus on the problematic of the state form of global capitalism. In turn, this allowed him to explore some difficult subjects in the emerging consensus over neoliberal governance, not least its embrace of a market-friendly vision of political correctness:

> '[an idyllic blond family leaving a suburban house] Narrator: Walter Schmidt: his family dropped bombs on this area for the Luftwaffe, but we don't mention that now because his firm's come to Milton Springsteen New Town. [a Japanese businessman playing golf] Narrator: Akio Takashiota: his father bombed Pearl Harbor, invaded Singapore, and strung up living skeletons by their thumbs for sadistic pleasure, but that's all forgotten now because his company's relocated to Milton Springsteen New Town. [a Sikh man] Narrator: Mehar Singh Gupta: his family fought and died for Britain in two world wars, but that's all forgotten now because with the new nationality laws, if he wants to come to Milton Springsteen New Town, he can just sod off. If he wants to live in Britain now, he'll have to bring a factory with him. Britain: where the past's been well and truly forgotten.'[12]

In this way, Sayle raises uncomfortable questions about the marketization of British immigration policy. On the one hand, it risks reproducing a naïve line about 'national' histories and their apparent moral relations to capital and the self; something akin to the nativist discourse of reactionary humour (albeit inflected with post-imperial solidarities). On the other hand, it points to a genuine tension in the emerging social democratic compromise over how to unite progressive values with global (and European) market reforms. Therefore, Sayle's personal struggle with alternative comedy might raise important questions for other, far more successful products of alternative comedy. In the movement from arts centres to comedy clubs and on to TV, Sayle (2016) lamented the 'selling out' of principle and the diminution of

---

[12] Sketch from *Alexei Sayle's Stuff*, which ran for three series on the BBC between 1988 and 1991. Downloaded from: https://www.youtube.com/watch?v=H5osSmOt9TU (accessed 27 July 2018).

alternative comedy to suit the 'Habitat shoppers' and '*Guardian* readers'. For his part, Tony Allen stopped appearing at the Comedy Store because of the 'career-oriented' focus of comedians, like Rik Mayall, Ade Edmondson, and French and Saunders, who all wanted to work on TV, which he saw as the 'greatest breakthrough in anaesthetic since chloroform' (see Schaffer, 2016: 380). More critically, Alex Sutton (forthcoming) argues that the embrace of liberal values in alternative comedy was accompanied by a formalization of liberal property rights; comedy became intellectual property just as acts began to distinguish themselves in terms of their 'identity', that is, the female comedian, the black comedian and so on. Thus, there is a commodification of the everyday life of the comedian, which qualifies any easy celebration of diversity. Indeed, as the UK sought to reinvent itself as 'open' and 'liberalized', the social democratic effort to compromise with globalization (in the name of growth and jobs) would witness a turn to favour this expansion of liberal rights, that is, the Third Way.

3 Alternative comedy 'is' politics

While certain acts resisted or otherwise struggled with commercialism, alternative comedy became broadly very successful. Ben Elton famously nurtured his links with the Oxbridge set to make four series of *Blackadder*, with *Blackadder Goes Fourth* marking a seminal contribution to popular revisionist histories of the First World War. More critically, this was a period when female and black comedians rose to mainstream prominence. While the comedy they produced may have veered from the uncompromising stances of Alexei Sayle or Tony Allen, the broad values of alternative comedy were progressively mainstreamed. The basic commitment to egalitarian politics of alternative comedy, anti-sexism, anti-racism, 'anti-Thatcher', was normalized and generalized through a commitment to diversity and inclusion, as well as a nebulous form of political correctness in broadcasting. How should we think about the politics of generalization? What possibilities and limits did it instantiate within the comic vernacular?

First, it is important to recognize the contribution that alternative comedy made to thinking about social diversity and inclusion. In terms of feminism, for instance, it is not just that women were 'added on' to the list of acts, but that they brought a range of substantive political subjects to the discourse of alternative comedy. For a long time, women in comedy had been constrained by a limited range of opportunities, partly through direct forms of marginalization practised by satire, for example men only clubs, and partly through the stereotyping female roles as housewives, objects of sexual fantasy, or 'ditzy' women

(Andrews, 1998). Instead, female alternative comedians not only practised comedy professionally, but did so 'outside' the usual roles allotted to women. Comedians like Victoria Wood, Jo Brand, and French and Saunders explored new themes like female relationships, sex (as something women can enjoy), and critiques of/within patriarchal gender norms, for example, Jo Brand's famous heckle response: "One of the reasons I keep the weight on is so that pricks like you won't fancy me." Emergent from the mainstreaming of female comedians and feminist issues was a self-conscious potential to foreground resistance to wider social and cultural norms. Indeed, this was a subject that had been openly courted in *The Young Ones*, with one scene witnessing Vyvyan smash through the TV screen to chastise *The Good Life* for providing a sickly heteronormative vision of Britain: "Felicity Treacle Kendal" and "sugar flavoured snob Briers"; a pair of "reactionary stereotypes confirming the myth that everyone in Britain is a loveable middle-class eccentric". On this view, gender was transformed from a punchline to a legitimating discourse of capitalist social relations.

Second, however, we should recognize the context and contingency of these issues in order to reflect on the consequences of commodifying alternative comedy. For all the progressive myths that surrounded alternative comedy, a curious set of dilemmas emerged from commodification itself (Sutton, forthcoming). Once the professional objective is established, that is, to get laughs, then comedy begins to occupy a liminal space where, for instance, we might wonder whether the 'aggressive feminist' comedian works as a resistance to gender norms or as a (newly acceptable) market variant of the female comedian? In this vein, Schaffer (2016) criticizes Dawn French's sitcom *Girls on Top*, in which French's *socialist feminist* character Amanda Ripley began to turn feminism into something like a farce. Editing a magazine called *Spare Cheeks*, for example, Ripley wrote a letter to Germaine Greer describing it as 'a magazine for women, by women, to women, of women, under women, about women, and basically a lot of other things to do with women type things'. Indeed, Ripley also ran seminars on how to 'know and understand your female toilet parts' and, on consecutive days, 'Women for power' and 'Women against power' (quoted in Schaffer, 2016).

Whether satirizing feminism is an ethical or political limit for alternative comedy is of course debatable. On the one hand, as the previous section argued, there is a wider politics of critique and dissent exemplified in Sayle's satires of the left, which emerged from genuine divisions between Marxism and social democracy. On this view, a vision of feminism which cannot laugh at itself, or critique itself through humour, would appear to miss the myriad instabilities and creative tensions that drive the feminist movement. On the other hand, we should try to take account of the productive and prefigurative possibilities of feminist satire. By establishing themselves in the mainstream of British comedy, French and Saunders inevitably provided an example that opened the way to new projects and comedians. Indeed, similar points can be made about the emergence of black and Asian comedians during this period. For instance, while elements of the early work of Lenny Henry can sometimes verge on the exploitation of black stereotypes, about being funny, cool, sexy and so on, the 'social fact' of having black comedians on shows like *Tiswas*, *OTT* and *The Lenny Henry Show* laid the groundwork for future black comedians to 'speak' the vernacular of comic resistance.

In short, mainstreaming matters. While Alexei Sayle decried the 'success' of alternative comedy and the wider structures of global capitalism that it legitimated through market-friendly progressive values, this should not distract us from the productive politics of comic resistance. Ubiquitous tropes of 'diversity' or 'political correctness' must be understood and evaluated in terms of what they allow, that is, a space in the mainstream of popular culture. As Stewart Lee argues, for all its ambiguities, political correctness means that violent, exclusionary and humiliating language is regularly pilloried or dismissed. The rise of alternative comedy meant that popular culture became a 'site' of global politics per se and this requires a new appreciation of the everyday politics of comic resistance.

On this view, a number of authors have pointed to the re-phrasing of the relationship between comedy and politics during this period. While it became clear that the vast swathe of anti-Tory satire made little dent on the success of right-wing governments and policies, alternative comedy nevertheless normalized the idea that comedians were credible political voices. Just as satire had generalized a certain sense of irony and wit in current affairs and investigative journalism, so alternative comedy brought a kind of authenticity to the progressive politics espoused by comedians. As Stephen Wagg (2002: 326) recounts, such authenticity is in high demand in mediatized society:

> Since the sixties, as Herbert Marcuse once said, the language of politics has become the language of advertising, and purveyors of satirical comedy have often been employed to assist in political communication. [...] Anthony Jay, writer of BBC Television's *Yes, Minister*, wrote speeches for Margaret Thatcher, and Stephen Fry periodically advised the Labour leadership on parliamentary performance. In

1996, when the comedian writer Mark Steel used his *Guardian* column to attack 'the pessimistic idea that the best we could hope for was Tony Blair', he was approached by Blair's front-bench colleague Robin Cook, inviting him to write jokes for his conference speech. (Cook's office was apparently unaware that Steel was a member of the Socialist Workers' Party.)

The increasingly symbiotic relationship between comedy and politics is not, however, a simple story of the triumph of form over substance. In performative terms, I would argue, it *produces new subjectivities and rationalities*. Just as the language of comedy became more 'right on', more egalitarian, even as it moved from the margins into the mainstream of globalized market life, it carried with it a set of resistant and satirical market subjects. While they may not have been capable of the pure form of revolution anticipated by Alexei Sayle, they nevertheless used the vernacular to articulate new political agendas that would further shape the critique of globalization. The interesting point about these performances is not so much about whether they achieved their 'goals' of resistance, but how the practice of identifying and engaging the ethico–political possibilities and limits of globalization became synonymous with comedy in British society. On this view, it is interesting to reflect on the work of people like Ben Elton. Widely derided as the chief 'sell out' of alternative comedy, he also played an important role in generalizing and normalizing the critique of globalization. While *The Man From Auntie* developed a typically watered down version of alternative comedy, that used observational humour to explore everyday issues of commodification, such as hairspray adverts where women suffered from 'head bobbing syndrome', he also explored more critical debates in his wider work. Indeed, his prolific writing ability saw him contribute to *Blackadder*, the fourth series of which mainstreamed a critical revisionist history of the First World War as a symptom of imperial arrogance; a growing disconnection between the upper classes and the lived experiences of the working classes sent to fight for their 'nation'. Moreover, he also wrote several novels, including *Stark*, which dealt with the question of global warming and how to resist it when large polluting corporations controlled the governments that might regulate them. In this book, he articulated (and satirized) the eco-Marxist critique of capitalism that the zenith of all economic growth is total planetary destruction.

Such a global imaginary was equally evident in the work of Lenny Henry. Working in standard sitcom and sketch formats, *The Lenny*

Henry Show both established the possibility of comedy with a mostly black cast, and allowed for the exploration of more radical ideas. For example, when his car is stolen it is suggested he calls the police, Delbert Wilkins replies: "Yeh sure, I'll call the police, like Nelson Mandela often calls up P.W. Botha when he fancies a nice chat." With contemporary eyes it's possible to look at some of Lenny Henry's work as a stereotypical portrayal of a young black man, who is over-confident, wearing loud clothes and loaded with 'street' phrases like 'wicked', and his own 'spondalitious'. In particular, one character, Joshua Yarlong, 'Africa's top pirate broadcaster', made high-pitched noises and said 'Katanga' a lot. Again, much like French and Saunders, the point is that Lenny Henry found a way into the mainstream, his comedy reflecting everyday life as someone who was black and British. His character Delbert Wilkins worked for the Brixton Broadcasting Corporation, an obvious play on the BBC, with guest radio hosts from all over the world. Once this diverse precedent was set, it arguably became far easier for broadcasters to 'imagine' and cater for a black audience through shows like *Desmond's* and later on, *Goodness Gracious Me.* Beyond straightforward comedy work, Lenny Henry even combined with Richard Curtis to raise money for Ethiopia initially, then developing countries across the world. Indeed, the rise to prominence of Red Nose Day arguably cemented the mainstream acceptability of alternative comedians as political activists, encouraging them to revisit the politics of British relations with developing countries through the prism of humanitarianism and a new global ethics of sympathy.

Conclusion

In conclusion, the chapter underlined how alternative comedy marks an important period for thinking about everyday comic resistance, as it pioneered a new vision of political comedy that embodied egalitarian values and (aesthetically) radical techniques. Alternative comedy politicized global market life by questioning the rapid changes associated with neoliberalism, articulating an everyday resistance to the legitimating narratives of individualism, self-interest and competition. While instrumental and critical frameworks can identify a clear set of limits – a failure to defeat the neoliberalism of successive Tory governments; the commodification of alternative comedy; and the racial and gendered limits of alternative comedians themselves (Schaffer, 2016) – a performative approach reflects how such ambiguities were precisely a focal point of concern in this more nuanced vernacular of resistance.

Thus, while ambiguities exist, not least in terms of success, commodification and the limited politics of generalization, I argue that such issues were a focal point *within* the 'movement'. Indeed, this is the point at which comedy can be more formally understood as a space of politics, rather than an agent. On this view, the chapter read the generalization of alternative comedy through the work and reflections of Alexei Sayle, arguing that we must contemplate the recuperation of resistance as both a limited and a (potentially) productive moment, allowing for the mainstreaming of female comedians, black comedians and new comic forms, such as revisionist histories, novels about the politics of global warming and so on. More critically, as the next chapter will consider, the symbiotic relationship between comedy and (global) politics would henceforth be a rich seam for ironic subversion.

4

Irony and the Liminality
of Resistance

Introduction: The anti-politics of irony?

British comedy has an acute potential to relay critical and reflexive arguments in the everyday public sphere of media entertainment. Previous chapters discerned an, *at first*, incidental, and subsequently, *far more* explicit association between comedy and radical politics over questions of imperial decline, class, the economy, commodification and so on. The contingent emergence of these central concerns within British comedy speaks of a sophisticated vernacular of everyday resistance that can both anticipate and negotiate the lived experiences of globalization. The potentialities of everyday comic resistance are sharpened by basic elements in the British satirical method; a sensitivity to (our own) pomposity, and a pervasive doubt about the grounds from which we joke, that is, self-deprecation. A democratization of this language through the rise of alternative comedy allowed for a rather more politicized and resistant inflection. Comedians actively contested the dumbing down of humour and thus the resistant qualities of the profession became a fundamental point of concern, one that recurs in in successive decades.

Leaving to one side the critical nuances of British comedy, this chapter will explore how the rise of 'irony' would fundamentally question the possibility of political comedy. Exponents of 1990s irony turned their attention to dilemmas of the 'self', very often a self that did not care about the 'serious' and 'boring' political issues that occupied alternative comedians. This emerged as part of a wider turn away from ideology associated with globalization and the (apparent) end of the Cold War. With the fall of the Berlin Wall and the so-called 'end of history', it was assumed that liberal cultural rights now formed an attractive normative consensus, so the question arose: why fight? Indeed, as Robert McCrum (2000) wrote in a sympathetic critique, it was far from obvious if irony was political at all:

> The ironic tone that now envelops the British media – what Umberto Eco called self-expression in inverted commas – is part of a sustained assault on seriousness for the purpose of populist entertainment. There is nothing wrong with a culture of ridicule in the face of overweening power, but when irony becomes the first, and sometimes the only mode of discourse, it clogs up the arteries of grown-up discussion. Irony and ignorance have formed an unholy alliance. [...] the British commentariat employs an ironic knowingness to disguise a real lack of knowledge. And in parts of academia, this ramshackle instrument is all the more lethal when referred to, approvingly, as 'postmodern'.

To underline, this is a sophisticated version of the instrumental critique, which questions the *generalization* of irony in British politics. It is important because it takes seriously the wider resonance of comedy across politics and society (including academia!). However, it also rehearses a problematic assumption that there is a 'correct' or 'proper' ontology of politics. As with other iterations of the instrumental approach, irony is again lamented as an impediment to 'grown-up discussion', a frittering away of liberal democratic freedoms. Against such an instrumental critique, this chapter will argue that 1990s irony manifested a more productive set of comic resistances that satirized the everyday lived experience of the emergent 'global market subject'.

While the irony period can be associated with a return of the 'everything is a target' attitude, section 1 argues that there are important critical nuances in the work of satirists like Chris Morris and Armando Iannucci. An increasingly intimate relation between satire and political communication became the central focus for Morris and Iannucci through defining shows like *The Day Today* and *The Saturday Night Armistice*. Emblematic here is Chris Morris's *Day Today*, which famously saw its news anchor engineer a declaration of war from a successful trade negotiation, triumphantly declaring: 'It's WAR!!' as a panoply of hyperbolic military reporting poured across the studio. In such satires, the locus of democracy is obscured by the rise of 24-hour news media, soundbite culture and gesture politics. Thus, I argue, the 'new satire' carried genuine critical insights about the emerging media form of global politics; how it can push political discourse in certain and limited directions (e.g. celebrity endorsement, moral panic and so on).

On this view, the everyday practices of globalization were actively subverted on their own terms, regardless of how such ironic resistance could be woven within a 'theory of politics' or reconciled with instrumental concerns for 'grown-up discussion' in state-centric models of global politics. However, despite such critical potentials, section 2 will identify important ambiguities in *the success* of irony. In particular, jokes about political correctness and multiculturalism in the work of Sacha Baron Cohen and Ricky Gervais seemed to perform a politics of offence for its own sake. The question recurred: was irony critical or reactionary? At one level, a generous interpretation might regard such humour as an everyday resistance to the hegemonic consensus, a subversion of the self-congratulatory discourse that diversity and political correctness can absolve globalization of its violence. At another level, however, by targeting the very liberal identity markers of multiculturalism so relentlessly, irony over political correctness could license a reactionary form of politics, whereby racist or sexist commentators could often absolve themselves with the phrase: "*I was just being ironic.*"

Drawing these points together, section 3 argues that ironic resistance is a liminal form that cannot be 'pinned down' in any neat way. Aspects of irony were clearly subversive, undermining the media form of global politics and presenting a new 'interactive' style of satire that embraced the productive potentials of the vernacular. On this view, if irony made us feel uncomfortable, it might be because it teased at genuine tensions in the politics of globalization; that diversity agendas and political correctness had not magically ended the gendered and colonial politics of market life. Indeed, this will be illustrated via a discussion of Ricky Gervais' contribution to Comic Relief that satirized the problematic politics of celebrity-driven global charity campaigns. However, the liminality of ironic resistance means that it must also take ownership of the capacity for jokes to close down any such reflection. Quintessentially, the sketch show *Little Britain* employed a form of irony regarding multiculturalism to 'celebrate' diversity through characters like 'the only gay in the village', the teenage chav Vicky Pollard, a transvestite who declared "I'm a Lady" even though she used the gents' toilet, and Ting Tong the mail-order bride (Lockyer, 2010). What the comedians saw as a celebration became problematic when repeated and recycled throughout society, a point that raises a fundamental and difficult question of responsibility.

1 Irony and the rise of new satire

The rise of 1990s irony, its success and generalization through commercial culture was widely regarded as a challenge to the ideals of alternative comedy. This echoed a wider concern on the left, a fear that postmodern relativism would encourage an 'anything goes' mentality, undermining the possibility of critical thought (Jameson, 1991). In this vein, Ben Elton sparked a war of words with *Loaded* magazine, a 'lads mag', which sought to refigure masculinity through a multi-layered, if non-serious, vision of constant reconstruction, that is, 1990s men could do the dishes 'and' fancy women. Ben Elton saw these 'postmodern ironic reconstructions of masculinity' as market-friendly 'porn mags', which encouraged readers to use irony to camouflage the fact that they were a 'mucky git' with an air of sophistication (Southwell, 1998). Typically, *Loaded* responded by writing articles about Ben Elton in terms of his 'crimes against comedy', arguing that he had long since stopped being funny and had become a whining old relic of the left.

Despite such pronounced oppositions, this section will argue that it would be a mistake to reduce ironic comedy to an uncritical acceptance of gendered (and raced) commodity culture. While 1990s irony can be associated with the swagger of acts like *The Mary Whitehouse Experience* and the lad mag hubris of *Loaded*, it also promoted a reflexivity among comedians as to the importance *and limits* of popular culture. As Stewart Lee (2010: 20) recalls:

> In 1993, Newman and Baddiel played Wembley Arena, where Rob Newman flew high up into the air on a wire whilst talking about how he liked Crass as a child. Janet Street-Porter saw a picture of this in *The Face* and declared 'comedy is the new rock and roll'. Suddenly stand-up looked like a career option for ambitious young people, and a cash cow for unscrupulous promoters. Could ye olde eighties Alternative Comedy still be 'alternative' when there were T-shirts of its latest stars on sale in skinny fit sizes at stadiums?

Beyond the noise and contradictions of instrumental success, there are important elements within irony that echo *and critically extend* the resistant potential of British comedy. Precisely by engaging the question of how comedy and commodity culture interact, I will argue, the emerging symbiosis between British comedy and everyday global politics could be politicized and resisted.

Indeed, the early work of Stewart Lee and Richard Herring (Lee and Herring) is an important illustration of the creative potentials of irony. From their overly literal interpretations of news stories by 'Lazy Journalist Scum' – for example, taking the headline 'Lee Evans Is Like Norman Wisdom on Acid' as an opportunity to give Norman Wisdom LSD and see if it's true – to their various reflections of the bizarre fit between reality TV and 'reality' – for example 'When Things Get Knocked Over, Spill, or Fall Out of Cupboards' (presented by Greg Evigan), or 'How Do They Do That?', a program about Channel Five executives who sit and watch clips of good television by other channels and ask: "*How do they do that?*" – Lee and Herring offered a form of comedy that was quite distinct. Well versed in the cultural tropes of the period, yet seeking a form of critique that worked within, rather than against their logics, this was not a simple sneer at market life. Instead, such comedy sought to inhabit the object of its satire: the media form.

This emerging milieu between comedy and media spectacle was also a productive moment for political satire. For instance, in *The Saturday Night Armistice*, Armando Iannucci presented a recurring sketch that played on a riff about how we come to know politics through personality: "Alright! … Fans of fans will be pleased to hear I met a clump of them this week in a drinking club devoted to perhaps the most popular man in Britain, certainly the most beautiful …"[1] The screen then segues to a report that looks at a group of fans cheering on their favourite politician Jack Straw down the pub – chanting, "I say, OOH-Ahh, Jacky Straw, say ooh-ahhh Jacky Straw!" Iannucci then enters the pub to interview the fans (the 'Straw dogs') about why they like him so much, "is it his politics?" – one replies: "everything about him … charisma, style, panache!"[2] In the following scene, they all go to Whitehall and try to see their hero, first met by a security guard, then Roy Hattersley and finally by Jack Straw, who seems genuinely pleased to have a fan club. They tell him how much they love him and show him their T-shirts with pictures of his face on, then get a selfie before he leaves.

The sketch highlights a vaguely suggestive possibility in irony. The basic joke is funny because of the (silly) juxtaposition between Jack Straw, a dull, straight-laced Home Secretary, and the exuberant, boisterous chanting of the fans. Indeed, you might even wonder: *is that it?* There does not appear to be a critique of Straw's political ideology

---

[1]   *The Saturday Night Armistice*, 22 July 1995, https://www.youtube.com/watch?v=pIVtS1CTzjw&#8230 (accessed 9 May 2020).
[2]   Ibid.

or policies, neither does it seem that he comes out of it particularly badly. Thus, it almost certainly fails the instrumental test of holding politicians to account. However, I would argue there is an open-ended quality to this style of sketch that can lead to far-reaching questions and resistances. For instance, the very idea of personality politics is magnified and made to look ridiculous. Someone who has so little charisma is literally cheered on as if he were a 'star player'. It teases at a growing use of 'relatability' in political communication under Tony Blair – who famously introduced a more personal style: jacket off, shirt sleeves rolled up, "call me Tony" and so on. Rather, than satirizing the politician for clear political reasons, Iannucci has identified and subverted the media form of their political presentation.

Moreover, there is an additional layer of ambiguity in that the fans are working-class men. Is the joke that they are not normally interested in politics? Is the joke that politics now tries to perform 'as if' it appeals to different social categories – Mondeo Man, for example? The difficulty of irony is that it leaves such possibilities open to interpretation. In another version of the sketch, a group of teenage fan girls show their love for Jeremy Hanley, because of *how brilliant* he is as Conservative Party Chair; they "trust him as an economist", know his majority off by heart, and think he has done "brilliant" work on restructuring the finances of the Conservative Party.[3] In both versions of the sketch, politicians seem happy to meet their adoring fans, indicating that – whether they are in on the joke or not – their media advisers are keen to engage new audiences. In this way, ironic resistance carries an interactive potential to ask open questions about *who we are* and how we come to know what politics is. While an instrumental critique might discern the fading of ideology, not least because the openness of these sketches allows the audience to think different things are funny, I would argue that these satires are prescient in their reckoning with brand engagement strategies and personality politics in the increasingly mediatized spectacle of global politics.

Chris Morris

The open-ended quality in irony is something that is picked up and developed by Chris Morris, who worked in a close collaboration with Iannucci on a number of ground-breaking and controversial shows.

---

[3]   *The Saturday Night Armistice*, 24 June 1995, https://www.youtube.com/watch?v=LYjTqOYbfig (accessed 9 May 2020).

Chris Morris is regarded as one of the true greats of modern satire. His uncompromising style, refusal to take part in the celebrity spectacle, and the tendency of other comedians to use and/or defer to his work mean he has an important place in British comedy akin to that of Peter Cook or Alexei Sayle. Often seen as prescient in his satire, a common refrain is to refer to any element of current politics as an unknowing reference to Chris Morris.

In line with Iannucci, Morris's satire developed by targeting the media form of politics. His early radio show *On the Hour* involved taking soundbites out of context, usually from leading politicians, or using sounds to identify the meaning of sections: whale sounds for the 'green news desk' for example. This absurdist style gradually developed via *The Day Today* to point to an important political limit in the news cycle: a need for sensation that diminishes the practical significance of policy and which may actually begin to set the agenda. In one sequence, coverage of the IRA's latest "theoretical strategy" of turning dogs into bombs, leads police to cordon off areas of London and conduct controlled explosions on (what the headline refers to as) 'Bombdogs' (later changed to 'Terrier-ists'). The menace of exploding dogs is juxtaposed with an interview with the head of Sinn Fein who is legally required to inhale helium when being interviewed "to subtract credibility from his statements".[4]

This combination of moral panic with (ridiculous) personality politics underpinned Morris's practice of interacting satirically with the world that came to fruition in *Brass Eye*. *Brass Eye* was a thematically organized news and documentary parody show that took a particular issue each episode and explored the problems and anxieties associated with the media's handling of that issue. In particular, 'Drugs' and 'Paedogeddon' develop a fascinating critique of everyday social life, while providing an innovative consideration of how important political concepts are known and represented in the public sphere. In performative terms, I would argue, the interesting point about Chris Morris is the way that his satire interacts with society and, subsequently, how mainstream politics attempts to take account of this.

Picking up where 'Bombdogs' left off, *Brass Eye* followed a method of ridiculing celebrated figures from the media, politics, sport and culture to show both the vacuity of celebrity, but also to contrast it with the weight and significance of the issues. For example, 'Drugs' features a number of celebrities, including Noel Edmonds, Bernard

---

[4]   *The Day Today*, 'Bombdogs', in episode 4, Stretchcast, 9 February 1994, https://www.youtube.com/watch?v=_nvfQw8UCDE (accessed 9 May 2020).

Manning, Rolf Harris, as well as the MP David Amess, who were asked to condemn and campaign against a drug called 'Cake', a new legal high from Czechoslovakia. Cake is represented by a large luminous tablet and the celebrities are told the tablet is "actual size", and are then asked to read out some fictitious scientific data about the drug.[5] Most famously, the campaign is organized by the 'Free the UK from Drugs' and 'British Opposition to Metabolically Bisturbile Drugs', or 'FUKD' and 'BOMBD' for short. In each interview, the celebrities are told of the (ludicrously) dangerous effects of 'cake' – including 'Czech neck', which inflates the neck so far that it engulfs the face causing asphyxiation, or Bernard Manning's lament that "one young kiddy on cake cried all the water out of his body" – as well as being asked to repeat regularly: "Cake is a made-up drug." However, nobody notices the joke and all are keen to stop the spread of drug use in the UK; indeed, MP David Amess's appearance on the show even led him to raise the existence of 'cake' in the House of Commons.[6]

By interacting satirically with the world, the programme highlights how easily the norm of celebrity campaigns oriented around moral panic can be subverted. Most famously, 'Paedogeddon' followed a similar format to 'Drugs'. Numerous celebrities were drafted in to make a series of absurd, yet emotionally charged, claims about paedophilia; from Phil Collins declaring that he was "talking nonce sense" (nonsense), to Barbara Follett MP talking about 'Pantou the Dog', a child's game on the internet where "an online paedophile has converted [the dog's eye] to be a webcam to look at the children playing".[7] Such games are said to be part of a Hidden Online Entrapment Control System, which is reduced to the acronym HOECS, said phonetically 'hoax'. Richard Blackwood states that such "HOECS games make your children smell like hammers" and that "online paedophiles can actually make your keyboard release toxic vapours that actually make you more suggestible". After sniffing his keyboard, he says, "Now I actually feel more suggestible. And that was just from one sniff."[8]

Again, it might be tempting to channel the instrumental critique here, for example, Lockyer and Attwood (2009: 57) make the point that *Brass Eye* does not offer any solutions, thus limiting how 'informative

---

[5] *Brass Eye*, 'Drugs', 5 February 1997, https://www.youtube.com/watch?v=MIAJemmO-bg (accessed 9 May 2020).
[6] Ibid.
[7] *Brass Eye – Paedogeddon Special*, 26 July 2001, https://www.youtube.com/watch?v=Q9frVTgoKSI (accessed 9 May 2020).
[8] Ibid.

or critical its satirical attack can be'. However, I would argue that the absurdity of *Brass Eye* not only satirizes the limited nature of British political discourse but also *deliberately performs it*. In so doing, Chris Morris clearly enters into an area of uncertainty (Meikle, 2012: 25). As he has reflected: "You have to be at best only half aware of what you're trying … if you know what you're looking for there's no attempt to do some real work" (in Hanks, 2000). On the issue of paedophilia, for instance, the *Brass Eye* episode (including the media reaction to the performance) performatively *embodied* the difficulty that British society has with paedophilia, not in spite *but because of* media and political interest in the matter. Uncomfortable as it may be, I would argue, the form of ironic resistance can entail a wider questioning and subversion of how we come to know (and therefore practise) global politics.

2 Ambiguities of irony: Ali G and Ricky Gervais

While the previous section made a qualified defence of the potential for irony to resist aspects of the mediatized form of global politics, this section will explore the potential limits of the form. There are clear ambiguities within irony that qualify its status as a form of political comedy in general, as well as the precise contours of its status as comic resistance, in particular. Indeed, as the previous section explored, the subversive performance of commodity culture seems to reproduce elements of that culture (albeit) in new ways. Any celebration of the open-ended and productive qualities of ironic resistance must therefore remain contingent upon the evaluation of unintended consequences. Even in the more sophisticated work of Iannucci and Morris, critics have argued, irony runs the risk of inhabiting the object of its satire so perfectly that it becomes indistinguishable. As Stephen Wagg (2002: 332) argues:

> Morris symbolically melts down all current affairs discourse and pours it into a pot marked 'Pompous'. In this he is the latest inheritor of the post-'TW3' paradigm of 'satire' that essentially licenses a suburban hostility to experts and politicians who are 'all as bad as each other'. This, in turn, feeds readily into a 'postmodern' acceptance of the futility of political intervention.

Although I disagree with the instrumental lament for proper 'political intervention', not least because of the broadening and deepening of *what it means to be political* that can be discerned in the work of

Morris (and Iannucci), it is nevertheless important to foreground and engage the potential ambivalences of irony. This section will examine the tensions that operate in the humour of Sacha Baron Cohen and Ricky Gervais. On the one hand, I will argue, their irony over political correctness can be read as *a critical resistance* to the Third Way moralization of globalization, questioning the normative consensus on political correctness and multiculturalism. On the other hand, their popularity also worked by courting a set of reactionary concerns with race, class and gender. Unlike the satire of Iannucci or Morris, it was commonplace for people to mimic the humour of Baron Cohen and Gervais in everyday life. This form of ironic resistance therefore carries a liminal quality, which raises a genuine dilemma: was the repetition of 'the joke' across popular culture actually part of a new process of legitimation as neoliberal market life recuperated and commodified the critique?

Ali G

Sacha Baron Cohen's character Ali G debuted in a set of short segments on *The 11 O'Clock Show*, but rapidly cut through with audiences to create successful TV shows in the UK and US, DVDs, a film, and (even) a cameo in a music video by Madonna. While aspects of Ali G's work can be seen in the same line of performative interaction pioneered by Chris Morris, one that can reveal instabilities and tensions across a range of social issues, an important departure was his emphasis on characterization. Ali G was a suburban teenage boy who played up his image and reputation as a gangster, a dealer and a sex symbol. For a UK audience, the joke was initially on him as he repeatedly riffed on the disconnect between the inflated idea he had of himself and the (obviously) lesser realities: his gang is the 'Staines Massiv'; his catchphrase is 'Boo-Yaka-Shah' (an apparent reference to 'junglist' DJs), he is 'West Side', though of course Ali G is referring to 'West Staines'. In 'da video' of his show, entitled *Innit*, short musical interludes portray Ali breakdancing in front of old people sitting in a shopping centre (he is bad, but styles it out by using gang signs).[9]

Much like the satires considered in the previous section, there is an open-ended quality to the humour. An important mechanism of the character's interaction with reality is the fact that Ali G is (deliberately) unintelligent, often misunderstanding the basic meaning

---

[9] *Innit*, 15 November 1999, https://www.youtube.com/watch?v=FyP-SMqJFsY (accessed 9 May 2020).

of words – for example, in an interview on education with Rhodes Boyson who advocates 'caning', Ali G thinks he means caning as in 'to get caned', that is, stoned.[10] This allows for a jarring affectionate tone in the interview despite the fact that Boyson is discussing corporal punishment. Again, it is unclear if we should laugh at Ali G's stupid mistake, Boyson's conservativism or, indeed, the cleverly crafted way in which Ali G reduces his own status to hoodwink Boyson? In this way, a combination of stupidity and exaggeration enable Baron Cohen to draw out and subvert social values, especially political correctness, by playing with participant (and audience) assumptions.

In visual terms, Ali G presents in exaggerated form; gold chains, orange tint Oakley sunglasses, brightly coloured track suits. He is essentially a caricature, a postmodern clown, whose character is able to identify and draw out ridiculous aspects of British society through a series of pranks (Saunders, 2009). While the basic joke is quite silly, often uncomfortable, Baron Cohen was skilled at creating a sense that there was always a step further to go:

> 'Britain is like a lady's punani, cos they is both made up of many parts. The [he whistles], the [he whistles in a higher pitch], and the [he clicks his tongue]. And if you was to keep the whole thing happy, you must pay proper attention to all of them. Which is why, me went to check out Wales, which me like to think of as the [high-pitched whistle again] of Britain, to help solve their problems. Check it.
>
> [A Welsh male voice choir sings over images of the valleys]
>
> 'When you hear the word Wales, you probably think of the fish with the biggest dick in the ocean, but it is also the name of a country that is only 200 miles away from Britain. They is all banging on about "a devolution", so I 'ave come 'ere to find out what it is, and if I can 'elp. West Side!'

	[He interviews Karl Davies of Plaid Cymru]
Ali G:	What does your boys want?
Karl Davies:	We want self-government for Wales.
Ali G:	So what 'appen if, you know, Blair go mental or whatever, and wanna come and invade the Wales, what will you do?

---

[10] Ibid.

Karl Davies:	We'd sing him away, hahaha!
Ali G:	aHAHAHAH [exaggerated]
	[He walks towards a mine]
Ali G:	Check dis, I is now going to a coal mine, which is a place where the Wales people used to live underground … Millions of years ago miners lived in here before they became human beings …[11]

The joke layers up pre-recorded segments to seem like a singular narrative of ever more absurd and ridiculous points. Britain is like a punani, which Ali G understands in terms of specific and related parts that he can only express in terms of whistles and clicks. He travels to Wales to find out what devolution is, but also to "help them". In this way, he performs a combination of acute misogyny, racism, and the arrogance of English imperial attitudes to Wales; comparing Wales to "the fish with the biggest dick"; narrating a backward nation that used to live under the ground before they "became human" and so on. Indeed, when he interviews a former miner in the pit and discovers they didn't actually live there, but chose to work down the mine, he remarks, astonished, "that is a … crap job!"[12]

In this way, Ali G was able to suspend critical judgement and take viewers through a line of quick and absurd jokes to positions that were uncomfortably funny. As a clown, he is able to express views that are violent and de-humanizing, even apparently in the company of genuine figures who seem to forgive his tactless insights. In the scene where he interviews a Welsh miner, he points to a picture of a miner who is covered in soot and asks "Why was they all brothers?", by which he means 'black men'; when it is explained they are white, he asks why was they "blacking up?"[13] At the time, these jokes went largely unremarked and while there were occasional allusions to the fact that Ali G was making a farce of black culture, the practical point remained that he was primarily clowning the suburban white kids who try to emulate black culture. The more offensive or misogynistic Ali G became, the more audiences seemed to enjoy watching celebrities take part: he had a talk show with interviewees like David and Victoria Beckham, who willingly participated to show they had a sense of humour. The idea was that if we could laugh at Ali G, then we could laugh at ourselves,

---

[11] Ibid.
[12] Ibid.
[13] Ibid.

even if (or because) it exposed the awkward persistence of national, racial and gendered hierarchies of power in a globalized Britain. This form of ironic resistance was therefore able to expose commitments to diversity and political correctness to a peculiar form of cultural transparency: could we (and celebrities) acknowledge our most violent selves through laughter?

The Office

While Ali G hinted at the possibilities of irony over political correctness, Ricky Gervais arguably took this form of humour in a far more pronounced and (eventually) controversial direction. Repeatedly, Gervais turns to the subjects of race, gender, physical and mental disability to nurture his acute irony over how liberal values hold together in everyday market life. Indeed, *The Office* is perhaps the seminal comedy of the irony period. The mockumentary style considers the experience of some increasingly desperate, bored and tragic figures who work in a paper company. While the set-up recalls the existential tone of earlier satires on the repetition of working life, the show magnifies the everyday irony of the period to challenge the liberal consensus of Third Way Britain.

If the economy was the centre of everything, then *The Office* was the appropriate stage for examining the dearth of social life. The merger between 'Slough' and the 'Swindon lot' is the tragic context within which Brent looks bad, first for promising to protect jobs (which he can't do) and then by elevating the status of the Swindon manager through his social charm and charity work. In the most famous scene, where Brent attempts to show that he is an equally good dancer (he is not), a humanist element arises. In the post-Fordist, flexible reality that underpins the British experience of globalization, managers are required to exhibit social skills, emotional labour, a GSOH (good sense of humour) and so on. This framing and subversion of the emotional labour required by Brent is just a small flicker of humanity in an otherwise bleak situation. Most fundamentally, the brutal irony of Brent is that he also pretends to hold the progressive values of the time, even though he clearly does not understand them, a conceit that allows *The Office* to explore older reactionary themes of British comedy, albeit with the perpetual ironic question as to where the meaning of each joke lay.

Much like the performative instability of Ali G's clowning, there is a liminality to the humour. On the one hand, the joke is clearly designed to make us laugh 'at' David Brent himself, with his misplaced self-belief that he is a great manager because he is a 'people person'. Quintessentially, he even embodies the British love of humour to define himself: "If you were to ask me three geniuses, I probably wouldn't say Einstein, Newton [he struggles to name a third] ... I'd go Milligan, Cleese, Everett ... Sessions."[14] Thus, his managerial schtick is to affect an everyman quality that he just does not possess. On the other hand, the show also teases at a set of more difficult subjects through Brent's palpable inability to understand or implement the progressive social values of the period. Thus, the humour emerges from scenes where Brent is trying to be politically correct, but all the time failing to appreciate the nuance or sensitivity of some of the ideas he is discussing.

Brent is regularly caught in questionable positions, trying to express ethical values, but more often collapsing into a clunky passion for one or other liberal identity marker, such as admiring Ian Botham because of his commitment to charity work – "Will you piss off and leave me alone, I'm walking to John O'Groats with some spastics."[15] On one of his many tours of the office, he finds an email picture of himself as a female porn star on someone's computer, which everyone finds funny. He addresses the whole office about the important issues:

'Well I'm angry, and not because I'm in it, but because it degrades women, which I hate, and the culprit, whoever he is, is in this room, *or she!* It could be a woman. Women are as filthy as men. Naming no names, I don't know any. But women are dirty.'[16]

In a similar vein, Brent tries to express his anti-racist beliefs in problematic ways, "I haven't got a sign on the door that says white people only, I don't care if you're black, brown, yellow – ye' cos orientals make very good workers actually." And when he is introducing the new temp to the office:

Brent:	This is Sanj, this guy does the best Ali G impression, Aiiieee. I can't do it, go on, do it.
Sanj:	I don't, must be someone else

14 'John Sessions shoutout on *The Office*', https://www.youtube.com/watch?v=gxUPgMCmtwg (accessed 10 May 2020).
15 *The Office*, David Brent's Life Philosophy, https://www.youtube.com/watch?v=u74UKFPzx78 (accessed 10 May 2020).
16 'David Brent Hates Sexism', https://www.youtube.com/watch?v=ye1C8vMqbHA (accessed 10 May 2020).

Brent: Oh sorry, it's the other one…
Sanj: The other what? … Paki?
Brent: Ah, that's racist.[17]

3 Towards a politics of liminality

Drawing these points together, the ethics and politics of ironic resistance are clearly ambiguous, if not unstable. This has led to charges that such comedy is 'too clever for its own good', that irony can act as camouflage for a more reactionary form of politics. Even if the characters of Ali G and David Brent are clowns, that is, figures we laugh at *because* they misconstrue the nuances of multicultural ethics, the open-ended nature of the humour invites polysemy (Weaver, 2011). In a word, the liminality of ironic resistance makes it hard to offer clear interpretations or normative assessments. Moreover, the rise to fame of Baron Cohen and Gervais introduces the problematic issue of *their own* circulation within global media culture.

This section will argue that the potential for a recuperation of irony within global media culture raises the question of responsibility, indeed, that the limits of ethics are actively mobilized and contemplated by comedians themselves. I articulate this discussion around some of the later work of Gervais, in particular, work that crystallizes the possibilities *and limits* of ironic resistance in global context. In particular, a short campaign video for the 2007 Comic Relief appeal opens with Ricky walking through a Kenyan village:

> 'I've been asked many times to come here to Kenya and I've always resisted it, probably because I was scared about what I might find, I thought it'd be too harrowing, and it is harrowing when half the country live in abject poverty, but despite the deprivation they don't just give up … they don't just roll over and sit around waiting for handouts. They do whatever they can to help themselves. They fight back.'[18]

The scenes behind Ricky involve Kenyans walking around in shantytowns with indigenous music playing in the background. He then meets Daniel Eboua who "like most Kenyans lives below the

---

[17] Excerpt from *The Office*, https://www.youtube.com/watch?v=Cir05JyEsV0 (accessed 27 July 2018).

[18] Ricky Gervais' African Appeal Comic Relief, 16 March 2007, https://www.youtube.com/watch?v=KK8I9106cfc (accessed 10 May 2020).

poverty line". They enter his house and Ricky points to all his worldly possessions, which amount to a few bags and old pots and pans, a fact which he says, "makes you feel spoilt, doesn't it? When we whinge about the things we whinge about." And then:

> Gervais: [Narrated] Even though Daniel has nothing, he wanted me to have one of his most prized possessions. [Spoken] 'He's just given me a cassette tape of U2.' [Narrated] And then came the sucker punch. Daniel: [Spoken] 'When my brother was in the hospital the doctor played him this cassette. The doctor was from England and he played this. I keep it because it reminds me of my brother. My brother died.'[19]

Ricky is visibly touched by this gesture and starts to cry. Some light music plays in the background, guitar chords from U2's 'One Love'. And Ricky assures him "it's not your fault". At this point Stephen Merchant walks in and the camera pans to reveal that everything has taken place in a film studio:

Merchant:	Alright Ricky what are you up to mate, what are you doing?
Gervais:	Just doing one of those Comic Relief appeals from Africa.
Merchant:	You're not in Africa though are you, this is BBC Television Centre.
Gervais:	Yeh, I don't actually have to go there do I?
Merchant:	You can't fake being in Africa.
Gervais:	Yeh, I can yeh. Get a blue screen, pop the hut up, Bob's your uncle.
Merchant:	No obviously technically you can fake it. You can't fake it morally.
Gervais:	Right, I'm not gonna go to a country where you need injections to get into it. That's not a good holiday. Also you get just as good publicity faking it as actually going there yourself. Everyone's a winner.[20]

---

[19] Ibid.
[20] Ibid.

To anyone familiar with Ricky Gervais' comedy what follows is standard stuff. Ricky ironically suggests that he is one of the world's greatest living comedians. He claims *The Office* "changed the genre" and compares himself favourably to John Cleese. He finishes with the suggestion of what people at home will think of him: "hold on though, we love everything he's done, but has he got a heart of gold? He's in Africa, the answer is yes! ... If he's doing that then we'll continue to buy his DVDs." Convinced of the argument, Steven Merchant decides to take part in the video. Then Jamie Oliver – who "hasn't been seen on TV caring about anything for at least 3 days" – also joins in. The progress is completed when Ricky sees a "homeless" "smack-head" that turns out to be Sir Bob Geldof. While Geldof initially describes it as a "fucking disgrace", he is eventually persuaded to take part because he has a single coming out. When filming is finished, Daniel takes off his mask to reveal that he is in fact Bono, dressed up as an African, attempting to promote the U2 singles album, which is coming out.

The ironic critique works in complex ways to make us question global aid campaigns. Similar to Iannucci's 'Theatre Aid' considered in Chapter 1, it subverts the various positionalities upon which global humanitarianism relies; both in the sense of a 'they' – the helpless recipients of cash, but more specifically, the idea of a 'we' (including the viewer who consumes their celebrity brand 'and' donates to Comic Relief). The sketch chastises the self-marketing and branding motivations of the celebrities who endorse global charity campaigns. Indeed, the layers of self-critique are highly sophisticated, at once problematizing our ability to 'know' the people we want to care for, while undermining the global pretensions of Western charity. For Gervais, 'their' place and culture can only appear as a caricature of humble native pride; he even admonishes Bob Geldof for swearing "in front of the ..." (he motions towards a Kenyan); thus playing upon a stereotype of child-like innocence. The fact that Gervais was able to explore such difficult and critical ideas in a short sketch that played during the Comic Relief campaign itself, suggests an ability to use irony in ways that promote an ethical conversation about what resistance might mean in global context.

More problematically, Gervais reprised David Brent in a more recent contribution for Comic Relief with the comedian/rapper, Doc Brown, called 'Equality Street'. This short vignette of 'political music' returns to themes of irony over political correctness to promote Brent's vision of multiculturalism, or as he defends it to Doc Brown: "it's perfect, cos its mega racial, but anti-racist":

Brent:	Let me take you down Equality Street, you never know the people you meet, at the end of the street is a golden gate, let in love, it don't let in hate, no. Walk with me down Equality Street, do unto others and life is sweet, books have no covers just look right in, you're judged by the words not the colour of your skin./ Day-o, day-o, me say day-o, biddlee bidlee bong yo!
Doc Brown:	Yo, I'm like John Lennon, except I do imagine there's a heaven, somewhere everyone is welcome, all my multicultural brethren. Where hate is outdated, today, love's the word, even for people from Luxembourg, or maybe like some other countries that you might ignore, Tonga, never thought of in my life before, but if I met a guy from Tonga then we'd stop and we'd speak, in fluent Tongalese on Equality Street, yep acceptance! See that Kenyan guy with mental eyes, he might be totally normal you can't generalise, Black People Aren't Crazy, Fat People Aren't Lazy, And Dwarves Aren't Babies! You can't just pick em up, they got rights, and anyway don't assume you could, they're not light! I learned the hard way ... Don't give a damn if you're Russian or Spanish, comrades, compadres, you can be a half gay woman with a dark face, one leg, no legs, long as you got a heart hey! Transgender, gay, straight, lesbians, whatever who ever, [to a gay skinhead] hey mate, let's be friends, but just friends. I want you to be, where you're properly free, obviously its Equality Street, believe, you know the deal there, everything is real fair, take a ride on my equal opportunity wheelchair.[21]

Such excerpts perform an acutely uncomfortable satire of multiculturalism. On the one hand, if you go along with the joke about Brent, then yes, he is still missing the point. The joke is somewhat elevated by the fact that Doc Brown is hugely unconvinced by Gervais as an artist, and indeed, has spoken about how his own character

---

[21] Brent and Johnson 'Equality Street', 15 March 2013, https://www.youtube.com/watch?v=XmTV62mE1PA (accessed 10 May 2020).

was also intended as subversion of egotistical rappers.[22] On the other hand, however, it risks playing to a more problematic set of debates over identity, where the subversion might be oddly reminiscent of the reactionary vision of difference, that values (or not) people entirely in terms of identity markers.

In broader terms, it is conceivable that circulating and repeating this joke acts to legitimate – or at least open a space for – a more mainstream critique of multiculturalism. Here we might think of the way someone like Jeremy Clarkson used *Top Gear* and his various newspaper columns for a kind of 'political correctness gone mad' agenda. Indeed, when *Top Gear* made a number of poor taste jokes about Mexicans and Mexican food, they defended their actions as 'just being ironic'. In response, Steve Coogan (2011) argued that 'real comedians':

> '[J]ustify their comedy from a moral standpoint. They are laughing at hypocrisy, human frailty, narrow-mindedness. [...] We are laughing at a lack of judgement and ignorance. There is a strong ethical dimension to the best comedy. Not only does it avoid reinforcing prejudices, it actively challenges them.'

Conclusion: Irony and responsibility

In conclusion, the liminality of ironic resistance can be both edifying and tranquillizing. While the instrumental critique portrays this ambiguity in terms of de-politicization, as a typically postmodern malaise that eschews any commitment to progressive satire, I have argued there is an important everyday politics of irony. In particular, the open-ended qualities of irony underpinned new forms of satire that reflected the rise and limits of the mediatized form of global politics. The everyday hierarchies of market life did not disappear as 'liberal triumphalism' might have hoped, a point both resisted and recuperated within ironic jokes about the limits of inter alia – the media form of global politics, multiculturalism and political correctness. However, the recuperation of irony was also productive of a certain set of reactionary possibilities that should be acknowledged. A good example of this essential ambiguity in irony is the extremely successful and more latterly controversial sketch show *Little Britain*.

---

[22] RHLSTP (Richard Herring's Leicester Square Podcast) with Ben Bailey Smith #104, 6 July 2016, https://www.youtube.com/watch?v=B_xvEQbBtEI (accessed 13 May 2020).

Little Britain developed a highly successful form of irony over multiculturalism that concentrated jokes into short and repeated sketches. The list of characters and subjects was a cornucopia of multicultural Britain, with a disabled man on benefits; Vicky Pollard – a chav schoolgirl; Bubbles, a black woman played by Lucas; Ting Tong, a mail-order bride; a couple of transvestites and so on. The point was to laugh 'at Britain', indeed, Matt Lucas has spoken of his desire to fully embrace the multicultural nature of Britain by laughing at these characters. Against the idea that this form of comedy could be perceived as 'punching down' at the marginal – for example, 'chav' is actually a social work acronym meaning 'council housed and violent' – Lucas has argued that the show was intended to be 'inclusive'.[23] He argues, for example, that ignoring a character like the Welsh gay ('the only gay in the village') would perform an exclusion from British society, indeed, that being part of the comic discourse is an important moment of national emergence.

While such arguments run the risk of essentializing what it means to be British, a point which the next chapter will discuss in relation to the turn against irony, Lucas identifies with a potential for ethical responsibility. Lucas's defence of the only gay in the village is heartfelt: as a gay man himself he felt like it was important to demonstrate a form of political agency through ironic self-deprecation. However, he has also spoken of the negative effects of the joke. By reducing the point to a simple catchphrase, the joke was able to circulate widely in British society. Indeed, he has recounted how people have written to him about it, to say they had been bullied with the same catchphrase.[24] Lucas's response has been to meet with such people and talk to them, to both explain and to apologize, indeed, affirming that many of the jokes would not be repeated now because of what he has learnt.[25] In this way, he hints at the kind of ethical and political responsibility that is required in irony, and the question of how and whether it might form part of the wider vernacular of comic resistance.[26]

---

[23] Matt Lucas, RHLSTP #214, 5 June 2019, https://www.youtube.com/ watch?v=4gL-dIFDxFA (accessed 10 May 2020).

[24] Ibid.

[25] Ibid.

[26] As Chapter 7 will discuss, an important and problematic question raised by *Little Britain* is the portrayal of non-white characters through 'blacking up', a form of performance with its own violent history within comedy, one which surely makes it harder to redeem through ideals of 'judgement' or the defence that 'it was ironic' (Malik, 2010).

5

Austerity and the Rise
of Radical Comedy

Introduction

British comedy took an essentially ambiguous turn through the 1990s and into the early 21st century. The complex layers of ironic meaning, critical distance, and reflexivity in relation to 'our' situation within global power relations served distinct functions. In the hands of satirists like Chris Morris, there was a subversive and potentially radical message: the mediatized form of global politics had prioritized spectacle, personality and soundbite. Yet, the popularity of ironic resistance, especially as it was developed by Sacha Baron Cohen and Ricky Gervais, created a moral dilemma: how far could – *or should* – irony go with questions of identity? A relentless focus on race, gender, disability and so on, might perform as reactionary when circulated for applause. As Stewart Lee (in Kovesi, 2012) reflected:

> 'in the 80s when alternative comedy started, one of the things that it was supposed to do was *not be* sexist, not make fun of people who were differently abled, not do racist stuff … […] A lot of it has crept back in under the idea that there's "irony"; that the comedian is holding up a mirror to society, *showing us our prejudices by enacting them for money.*'

This is a clear ethical limit for irony. While Gervais may be capable of articulating the distinction between the 'subject of social violence' and 'the joke he is making about that violence', it is unclear whether this nuance is always operative with the audience. As such, Chapter 4 made a qualified argument that the liminality of ironic resistance worked to foreground questions of responsibility. Although some jokes may be subversive, for example Gervais' satire of global charity campaigns, similarly ironic jokes can perform a moment of exclusion – *Little Britain* for example. Indeed, the next chapter will question how the (re-)emergence of right-wing and reactionary comedy has begun to explore ironic themes, albeit from a libertarian position on free speech. However, for now, this chapter will explore a more radical turn in British comedy associated with the work of comedians like Charlie Brooker, Russell Brand and Stewart Lee.

While aspects of the radical turn can be understood as a 'push back' against the exclusionary possibilities of irony, not least Stewart Lee's (2009) defence of political correctness, it is also important to recognize and situate radical comedy within the everyday experience of global crisis. After liberal triumphalism and the Third Way moralization of globalization that served as a backdrop for the rise of irony, the global political events that marked the return of radical comedy were the War on Terror, the Global Financial Crisis (GFC) and the rise of austerity. In this vein, several comedians returned to the ideals of alternative comedy as well as the satirical techniques of Chris Morris to articulate a far more engaged vision of comic resistance.

From the sophisticated satire of government in the age of mediatized politics of *The Thick of It,* to the fast-paced deconstruction of the global news agenda in Charlie Brooker's *Newswipe*, satire discovered its capacity to challenge both the saccharine and the ironic portrayal of neoliberal market life. With the GFC and the rise of austerity, comedians like Russell Brand and Stewart Lee began to explore the radical potential of stand-up, inflecting their humour with ideas of revolution and questions about the market self in late capitalism. Thus, the substance of radical comedy reinvented the 'anti-establishment' tradition via a critical engagement with the everyday performance of neoliberal globalization.

This argument is developed over three sections. Section 1 will look at the sharp subversion of government that accompanied the end of the Blair governments and the growing politicization of 'spin'. In particular, *The Thick of It* provided a deconstruction of the competing and conflicting logics of mediatized global politics; in the process of spinning, politicians and their advisers moved further and further from the everyday life of people. This critical perspective on the logics and rationalities of global politics was echoed in the work of Charlie Brooker, who pointed to the rise of affect in the media relay, with its projection of vast existential crises via everyday tropes and metaphors. In shows like *Newswipe*, I argue, Brooker provides a radical re-description of the ironic focus on the self, one that might recover the contingency of agency within neoliberalism.

Section 2 engages the work of Russell Brand and Stewart Lee, arguing that – in different ways – they each articulate a form of comedy that borders on an everyday 'theory' of resistance. For his part, Brand extended the 'anti-establishment' line by pointing out how representative democracy *actually entrenches* corporate interests. Channelling popular disillusionment with austerity, his comedy can sometimes appear as anti-elite point scoring, yet I argue that his wider political thought and activism suggest a more radical potential. These themes are developed in the work of Stewart Lee who, while openly critical of Brand, regularly engages the question of his own positionality within global capitalism. By actively questioning the performativity of the satirical market subject, through everyday discourses of capitalism like *Scooby Doo* and advertising, Lee provides a reflective moment on how global politics hangs together '*through us*'.

Finally, section 3 points to certain limits and unintended consequences in radical comedy. To underline, there is something deeply engaging about the weaving of comedy with radical themes of mediatization, subversion of the market self, and radical democracy. Neither an apology for Britain's hegemonic role within globalization, nor an ironic disavowal of ethical responsibility, radical comedy is an important discourse on everyday agency in global politics. However, there are also important limits in the performance of radical humour. On the one hand, instrumental and critical frameworks see a diminution of political practice, quite famously in Russell Brand's advocacy 'against' voting, but more profoundly in the centrality of (a heroic?) masculinity to radical comedy. Simply put, for all the reflexivity to contingency, once again, this period produced a series of 'strong' white male comedians. On the other hand, I will suggest a more pervasive consequence in the popularity of radical comedy: the generalization of satirical literacy. This period saw rapid technological changes that facilitated everyday market subjects to engage in (global) politics through satirical hashtags and memes (Dean, 2019). In the process, the ongoing symbiosis between comedy and politics began to take account of the productive agency of the audience itself: the citizen satirist.

1 Everyday politics of 'the system'

The rise of radical comedy can be situated alongside the decline of (support for) Third Way politics. While Blair had engaged the 'opportunity' of globalization in terms of managerial discourses of 'governance', the substantive handling of information during the War on Terror and the GFC rapidly combined to make tropes of 'transparency' and 'accountability' seem disingenuous. Indeed, the emergence of post-truth politics is prefigured by growing doubts over the honesty of political elites during this period. Keynote incidents such as the 'dodgy dossier' used to justify intervention in Iraq; the massive public funded bail-out of the banks, which led to austerity; and the MPs' expenses scandal that juxtaposed austerity for the many with MPs' claims of, for example, £1,600 for a duck house – combined to undermine popular faith in politics and politicians. In this context, an important precursor of radical comedy can be found work of Armando Iannucci and, more directly, in Charlie Brooker. In different ways, they each developed satires of how we come to know politics, in the process subverting many of the cherished assumptions that underpin representative democracy: transparency, accountability and (economic) expertise. More critically, they achieved this through an augmented vision of satire that directly hailed the experiences and feelings of the everyday market subject who 'viewed' global politics.

If Chris Morris asked a set of interesting performative questions about the mediatized form of politics, where sensation and celebrity culture combine to make politics look faintly ridiculous, *The Thick of It* developed a more formal set-up: what happens when we make this absurd situation the fundamental context of public policy? Indeed, going beyond his open-ended and playful satires considered in the previous chapter, Armando Iannucci used the *The Thick of It* to crystallize how different rationalities overlap to produce a pervasive – *and self-undermining* – logic to 'the system'. Importantly, this satire unfolds on the mundane terrain of the lived experiences of the politicians themselves, and thus, the everyday becomes a productive resource for critical reflection. In one early scene, Hugh Abbott struggles to keep up:

> 'I work, I eat, I shower. That's it. Occasionally, I take a dump, just as a sort of treat. I mean, that really is my treat. That's what it's come to. I sit there and I think, "No, I'm not going to read *The New Statesman*. This time is just for me. This is quality time just for me." Is that normal?'[1]

---

[1] *The Thick of It*, 'Quality Time', 19 May 2005, https://www.youtube.com/watch?v=b4AoSBqY_GI (accessed 11 May 2020). Hugh Abbott is the first Minister for Social Affairs in *The Thick of It*, eventually replaced by Nicola Murray. He explains his "treat" to Glenn Cullen, who acts as his dogsbody throughout the

Equally, in the heat of political crisis, Peter Mannion goes for a Twix and, at another point, Malcolm Tucker demands a Curly Wurly (a classic one though, because "a Curly Wurly should be the size of a small ladder").[2] This humanizing quality in *The Thick of It* allows for a reflexivity regarding the inhuman nature of the stresses and strains of life in politics.

The politicians ostensibly sit at the top of a cast of unelected special advisers and civil servants, yet it soon becomes clear they live and work in constant fear of the media cycle, as it is embodied and produced by 'spin doctors' like Malcolm Tucker. Indeed, the political agency of politicians is often quite diminished; swamped by efforts to pander to the media cycle. For example, Peter Mannion struggles to understand the very concept of an app when trying and failing to sell his coalition partner's vision of a "silicon playground".[3] All he can remember is the empty phrase "I call app Britain" (supposedly a play on 'I call up Britain') and ends up talking in circles about "digital dividends" to a room full of tech-savvy school children.[4] It is a policy he does not understand, does not want to promote, and – through a comedy of errors – one he even destroys *against his will*.

In policy terms, government is constrained, not principally by action or deed, but by public perception and the tortuous process of *attempting to constitute* that perception. Even if the characters recognize the dynamic, they can find no comfort, because all their interventions perpetuate new problems. The apparent master of spin, the abrasive Malcolm Tucker – "Come the fuck in, or fuck the fuck off" – tries but often fails to keep ahead of the media cycle. From pre-emptive leaking that their focus group has been using an actress (which turns out to be unnecessary because she hasn't told the media as they had feared); to managing the perception of equality by placing Nicola Murray's child in a state school (where she goes off

---

first two series. Glenn, in response to Hugh's rhetorical question, answers, "It's sad." Hugh retorts: "Well, at least I've made something."

[2] *The Thick of It*, 'Curly Wurly', 28 November 2009, https://www.youtube.com/watch?v=Byk6KNC9nvc (accessed 11 May 2020).

[3] Peter Mannion, the Tory Minister for Social Affairs and Citizenship in a Coalition government, launches a policy to get students to design apps in classrooms, for which they would not be paid. Mannion, completely out of touch with both technology and social change in Britain, embarrasses himself and the government at the launch. This fictional policy reflected – and in fact, preceded – a policy implemented by the actual Coalition government in 2012.

[4] *The Thick of It*, 'Silicon Playground', 8 September 2012, https://www.youtube.com/watch?v=ZnKYAmdXWb8 (accessed 11 May 2020).

the rails and becomes a potential nightmare headline for the government), his intensity often backfires. This diminution of political agency therefore creates a larger question about how the system actually works; how the mediatized context of politics has become a self-perpetuating edifice.

Along the way politicians lose their jobs, policies are jettisoned (or gutted to the point of being meaningless), and all the while, people try frantically to hang on to their sanity.[5] Even Tucker, that most Machiavellian figure of power, eventually succumbs. At one point, in a public dispute with Terri, she tells him he is losing it and he should apologize. In response, he leads her into a private room for what looks to be an apocalyptic dressing down, but instead, his breakdown continues, and he actually opens up about the pressure he is feeling. When Terri comforts him and apologizes, he reassures her:

> 'No, I'm over it, okay? Don't you apologise. Don't you fucking apologise. You don't need to apologise. I love this place. I do. I mean, fucking, compared to Number 10, this place is fucking tranquil, yeah? Over there, 300 yards down the road, I mean, it's like a fucking cancer ward. I mean, there are people in there, they're fucking screaming at each other. They are screaming, "You gave me this fucking disease." "You gave me this fucking disease." And every corner that I turn there's another threat, Terri. Hacks, hacks, fucking vampire hacks. And they're slaughtering us, Terri. They are fucking slaughtering us and they want my face for a flannel! And you know what? I used to be the fucking pharaoh, Terri. I used to be the fucking pharaoh. Now I'm fucking floundering in a fucking Nile of shit. But I am going to fashion a paddle out of that shit. Yeah?'[6]

5   Elements of this story are deeply tragic; for example, Douglass Tickel, a nurse camped outside Parliament in opposition to government policy, is regularly derided by the members of the Coalition government and the opposition, not least because his name makes him sound like a *Mr Men* character. Tickel's story is the driving force and instigation for all the events of the final series, even leading to the final downfall of Malcolm Tucker, who leaks his medical records.

6   *The Thick of It*, 'Terri Takes a Tuckering', 28 November 2009, https://www.youtube.com/watch?v=hjo0f_O6Pac (accessed 11 May 2020). Terri Coverley's role in the Department for Social Affairs and Citizenship is to manage media relations. She is the former Head of Press for Waitrose and, ostensibly, the least competent at her job. She is not respected at all by her colleagues in the department. For this

It may be tempting to channel the instrumental critique, to dismiss the cynical dimensions of the *The Thick of It*. For example, Fielding (2014a: 260) describes the programme as 'denigrating popular agency' through its depiction of the public as uninterested and overly critical towards (self-serving) politicians. However, I would argue that, to some extent that is the point: to expose how the very idea of 'the public' has become relegated to a nodal point in the system; something to be 'nudged' or otherwise patronized with soundbites and media-friendly narratives.

In one scene, Peter Mannion is confronted by a woman who has to care for her mother, who is upset because she has to clean up her piss, asking Mannion (in front of TV cameras): "Have you ever had to clean up your own mother's piss?" By juxtaposing the everyday life of a carer, who lives at the sharp end of welfare cuts, alongside the futility of Mannion's own diminished agency: "Look, can you just stop saying piss?!", the constraining logics of the political system are writ large. Far from a cynical view, I would argue *The Thick of It* provides a basis for a radical critique of representative democracy, where separations between politicians and public are entrenched as part of the operating mechanism of politics via strategies to 'better communicate' (for example, with 'quiet bat people'). Much like the discussion of 'fans' in *The Saturday Night Armistice*, Iannucci has found a way to represent the mediatized form of politics in order to reveal something: a critical lens through which the distinction between politics and everyday life might be re-politicized.

Charlie Brooker

Building on this satirical system, Charlie Brooker uses a combination of crafted text and quick visual sequences to portray a media narrative that has run away with its own importance. His style might be typified as high snark, or thoughtful buffoonery, in that it undercuts the superficiality of mainstream politics, but is nevertheless capable of using sexual innuendo to punctuate it. In this way, Brooker embodies elements of the irony period, while allowing his satire to be led by events. Indeed, the timing of Brooker's *Newswipe* means that large tracts of his satire have been targeted at issues relating to the global financial crisis and the politics of austerity. In one sequence, he pulls apart news

---

reason, it is particularly unusual that Malcolm Tucker, of all people, should confide in and sincerely apologize to her. She offers him a hug, which he declines.

coverage of the GFC through a critique of the melodramatic discourse of the economy:

> 'Unemployment now so huge it has to be depicted by plummeting monolithic numbers. [...] The news itself is becoming less of an easily digestible summary of events and more a grotesque entertainment reality show with heavy emphasis on emotion and sensation and a swaggeringly comically theatrical sense of its own importance ... [...]'

Jeremy Paxman: Today stock markets across the world tumbled, imploded, continued to collapse like deflated dirigibles.

Brooker: After all if the boom of the last decade was all a dream the current situation is a nightmare rendered in calculus, meaninglessly huge numbers, sliding graphs, a CGI Red Arrows display team crashing repeatedly to the floor, and one frightening prognosis after another. It's so bad leaders of the G20 are having to get together in the world's most disappointing razzle pile-up in a desperate bid to save the world from global cash-pocalypse. [...]

> 'Of course, the news hasn't been too scared of using the current financial mess to pad out their bulletins. On a slow news day you can tie almost any story into it. It's the gift that keeps on giving. You can shoot out some chirpy guff about feeding your pets on a budget.'

GMTV: Don't worry about spending lots of money on tasty treats cos dogs are actually far happier with something simple like a nice raw carrot.[7]

In the same sequence, Brooker then parodies the litany of flawed metaphorical devices used to explain quantitative easing: these include spanners, petrol cans and railway tracks. To cap off this performance of the global economy, he introduces Dermot Murnaghan's 'Economic

---

[7] *Newswipe with Charlie Brooker*, Series One, episode 1, 25 March 2009, https://www.youtube.com/watch?v=B63ahmTAesM (accessed 11 May 2020).

Cycle', where Dermot 'rides a bicycle' around England attempting to interview individuals affected by the downturn in the 'economic cycle'. Unfortunately, the majority of people interviewed were actually doing pretty well and were mildly optimistic about economic prospects.[8]

In this sense, Brooker goes a stage further than Iannucci by foregrounding the reflexive nature of the viewer subject. The form of the satire, which uses actual news coverage of the GFC, is crucial here, because it challenges how everyday knowledge about the global economy is actually produced. Brooker's incredulity at the grand, apocalyptic stories of the economy, told from his comfortable sofa, while he 'talks to the telly', work to satirize how everyday market subjects learned about the GFC. Indeed, in another intervention, Brooker goes further to look at how mobilization of affect during the crisis became a staple of media coverage of austerity. In particular, he addressed a critical public debate over *Benefits Street*, a Channel 4 documentary about 'real life' in austerity Britain:

> 'In order to function without exploding, [...] British society seems to require a regularly updated register of sanctioned hate figures, about whom it's OK to say more or less anything [...] The current list includes paedos, MPs, immigrants, bankers, people on benefits and reality stars. Some of the *Benefits Street* cast falls into the final two categories simultaneously, which means hatred squared.' (Brooker, 2014)

Brooker makes an interesting link here between anger and the social legitimacy of the market. Counterintuitively, neoliberal market reforms rely fundamentally on a sense of society, even as they seek to unpick any notion of state support for that society. Sometimes this sense of society is maintained through war, or profit, but in a downturn (as per the 'cash-pocalypse') anger is more often mobilized. In this way, Brooker is addressing the audience of media: the individual subject, who watches the news and seeks to comprehend global events. This is important because it speaks to themes in the everyday turn about how subjects are required to take on board and reproduce certain rationalities (Langley, 2007; Seabrooke, 2010).

Beyond the presenter and the narrator, Brooker also appears as a television viewer, sat in his living room on a comfortable sofa. This attempt to define and personalize the audience suggests a degree

---

[8] Ibid.

of identification – breaking down the illusory barrier between performer and audience – and a provocation, asking us: Do you see it this way? Do you challenge or question what you are told? Such a reflexive conception of the audience-subject suggests an unstable performance: there is a possibility for disagreement, ignorance, denial, or even involvement. Indeed, in his satire of *Benefits Street*, Brooker developed two additional viewer characters – Barry Shitpeas and Philomena Cunk – who comment upon and engage in the various politico-media narratives that are emerging. The irony in these talking head vignettes is often multi-layered and difficult to pin down, a fact that brings a rich, polyphonic experience to the satire. In one discussion, they take Brooker's theme of anger one stage further:

Barry Shitpeas: There was this sort of anger-making programme called *Benefits Street*. It gave you a fascinating insight into the lives of these people who've got next to nothing, so you can judge 'em. [...]

Philomena Cunk: When I was watching it, I felt sort of pity for the people in it, but when I went on Twitter everyone was angry with them so I thought, oh I've got it wrong I'd better join in with that, so then I wrote these little tweet things, about how they were scum and bastards and about how I hope the government fucking shoots them, and then stands over their bodies pumping bullet after bullet into their benefit scum bastard bodies. And I got like 20 new followers for that so it was a pretty good program.... People say there's no community anymore but watching that interesting show and joining in with everyone on the internet hating them together, sort of outdoing each other to express how much hate you felt, was amazing. I don't think I've ever felt so much part of a huge group with all this fun anger surging through us. It really made me feel alive.[9]

By placing the viewer at the centre of the satire, there is a challenge to think through how the mediatized form of global politics works,

---

[9] *Charlie Brooker's Weekly Wipe*, 'Benefits Street', 16 January 2014, https://www.youtube.com/watch?v=KUYEk5nRlFw (accessed 11 May 2020).

where opinions come from, and how they are disciplined. The person who watches Charlie Brooker is performatively inscribed as both the recipient and the instigator of the satire. Beyond questions of getting the joke or not, liking it, or not, a performative instability is presented as the centre of the experience: how do we come to know *and therefore make* global politics?

While such humour could go in a number of directions, Brooker's perpetual return to the GFC and the confused politics of austerity was taken in a radical direction by his inclusion of a piece by Adam Curtis in his *Yearly Wipe*. In it, Curtis elaborates upon Brooker's themes of bewilderment at the "chaos that seems to be engulfing everything". Across a combination of disjointed sequences and a typically dystopian lo-fi soundtrack, Curtis describes an "odd non-linear world that plays into the hands of those in power", where everything the media tells us seems confusing and contradictory. We have the biggest financial crisis in decades, yet not a single banker goes to jail. Instead, they get bailed out and given millions in quantitative easing:

> 'But it gets even more confusing because the Bank of England has admitted that those millions of pounds have not gone where they are supposed to. A vast amount of the money has actually found its way into the hands of the wealthiest 5 per cent in Britain. It has been described as the biggest transfer of wealth to the rich in recent documented history. It could be a huge scandal comparable to the greedy oligarchs in Russia. A ruthless elite syphoning off billions of pounds in public money. But nobody seems to know. It sums up the strange mood of our time where nothing really makes any coherent sense. We live with a constant vaudeville of contradictory stories, which makes it impossible for any real opposition to emerge because they can't counter it with a coherent narrative of their own. And it means that we as individuals become ever more powerless – unable to challenge anything because we live in a state of confusion and uncertainty. To which the response is "oh dear". But that's what they want you to say.'[10]

---

[10]   *Charlie Brooker's 2014 Wipe – Non-Linear Warfare'*, 30 December 2014, https://www.youtube.com/watch?v=KOY4Ka-GBus (accessed 11 May 2020).

2 Comedy as political theory: anti-capitalist, radical democracy

While not explicitly radical in spirit, the satirical work of Iannucci and Brooker consolidated earlier ideas in the work of Chris Morris to focus on the mediatized form of politics. Crucially, however, rather than simply elucidating the absurdity of public spectacle, they each foregrounded the politics of the everyday, how representative democracy had come to rest on logics that both separated out and sought to discipline market subjects. From a tragic mood in *The Thick of It* to a vaguely conspiratorial gesture at post-GFC austerity politics in Brooker, the hailing of an everyday market subject is identified as a crucial element in sustaining 'the system'. This section will now consider the work of Russell Brand and Stewart Lee as two radical comedians who portray a similar ontology of global politics-as-systemic, while refiguring the everyday market subject as an agent of both discipline *and* resistance.

Russell Brand

Russell Brand occupies an interesting place in British comedy. His technique combines an extrovert personality with free form, stream-of-consciousness style engagements. Despite the 'novelty' of his style, the humour tends to revolve around a standard mix of self-deprecation and absurd or exaggerated points of comparison. However, he is an important figure because of his explicit turn to radical politics, both in his personal actions – drug use campaigns, G20/anti-austerity protests, highlighting Hugo Boss's links to the Nazis and so on – and in his comedy material. Shows like *Messiah Complex* (2013, filmed at the Hammersmith Apollo) have focused on the question of inspirational political leadership, while his daily video, *The Trews*, presented critical analyses of advertising, news coverage and Israeli aggression in the Middle East. Perhaps most famously, Brand appeared in a high-profile interview on *Newsnight* where he outlined his principal critiques of state-level democracy and called for a popular revolt against the system.

In this way, Brand developed a sustained critique of the state form of global politics and its role in upholding structures of domination and inequality. Importantly, he located his critique in terms of the imaginative narrative of politics, the media discourses that present stories about 'heroes and villians', which inculcate fear and secure support for the system. For example, in *Messiah Complex* (2013), he satirizes media coverage of migration for essentially shouting the word 'immigrant' repeatedly, and asks *Fox News*: "you do know that an immigrant is just someone who used to be somewhere else don't you?" This point is exaggerated to absurdity to illustrate the contradictions of a sovereign world-view; mockingly taking on the persona of *Fox News* he says to the immigrant:

> 'I want you stay in the same place on this sphere that is floating in infinite space, this sphere with arbitrary and artificial geopolitical boundaries drawn upon it. Stay put, in the same place, and don't move. Don't think about global capital flows that move to meet the demands of western consumers, don't think about how they will put similar demands on the movement of labour. Just stay still!'

Of course, this notion of media critique is personal, and reflects an ongoing fascination that Brand has with *his own place* in the spotlight. For instance, during anti-austerity protests he addressed the crowd to note that when he was poor and criticized capitalism, he was told it was because he was just jealous, yet when he was rich and criticized capitalism, he was told he was a hypocrite. So maybe it's just that people don't like him criticizing capitalism? But perhaps the keynote intervention was made in an interview with Paxman, where Brand melded his critique of state-level politics to the media's ability to legitimate Westminster.[11]

In the interview, Brand subverts the paradigm of parliamentary democracy for upholding the privileged interests of a ruling class, and for being complicit in processes of ecological degradation and the creation of an underclass. When Paxman pushes him on standard political lines, he clearly states that he never votes and urges people not to vote for MPs who are complicit in a system that creates inequality. He claims to look beyond the pre-existing paradigm for alternatives and he argues for a revolution to create a socialist egalitarian system with a massive redistribution of wealth. And when Paxman pushes him on whether people could possibly take him seriously, he says, "I don't care if people take me seriously", highlighting that there are plenty of serious politicians who haven't changed anything: "at least being facetious is funny".[12]

---

[11] *Paxman vs. Russell Brand Full Interview – Newsnight*, 23 October 2013, https://www.youtube.com/watch?v=3YR4CseY9pk (accessed 11 May 2020).

[12] Ibid.

Finally, Brand turns the discussion to subject positions, allowing an affective turn in the argument. He highlights Paxman's place within the system, first by drawing attention to the curious image of a BBC presenter who berates politicians for most of his career and never gets tired that nothing changes, and, second, by drawing attention to Paxman's own emotional stake in the suffering caused by class and hierarchy. When Paxman says, "I'm surprised you can be facetious when you're that angry", Brand replies:

> 'Yes I am angry, I am angry, because for me it's real. It's not just some peripheral thing that I turn up to once in a while ... for me this is what I come from, what I care about. [...] There's gonna be a revolution, it's going to happen ... this is the end.... I remember I see you in that programme where you look at your ancestors, and you saw the way your grandmother had to brass herself, or got fucked over by the aristocrats who ran her gaff, you cried because you knew that it was unfair and unjust, and that was, what a century ago? This is happening to people now ... so if we can engage that feeling instead of some moment of lachrymose sentimentality trotted out on the TV for people to pore over emotional porn. If we can engage that feeling and actually change things, why wouldn't we?'[13]

Stewart Lee

If Brand points to the emotion of change, and Brooker points to the way anger can be used to legitimate neoliberal restructuring, then Stewart Lee extends the critique to expose a dilemma between (the very possibility of) meaning and market subjectivity. Stewart Lee is on a comic level above Brand and Brooker; he is arguably one of the finest stand-up comedians in British comedy. His style is one of perpetual deconstruction, irritation and absurdity. The incongruous mix of pedantry, anger and – by Lee's own admission – his turn to inserting material that *simply is not meant to be funny*, means that there are often several ways in which the humour can be understood.

In his show *Carpet Remnant World* (2012) he builds an anti-joke around a narrative of boredom, about being a dad, who drives around to gigs all the time and watches *Scooby Doo* films with his son. In

---

[13] Ibid.

particular, he has watched *Scooby Doo and the Zombie Pirate Jungle Island* "152 times!" Perpetually dividing his audience between the clever ones who get the joke and "new people" who've come because he's on the TV now (who he politely warns: "I'm not like Michael McIntyre, I haven't noticed anything in your lives") – he then presents a satire of Tory cuts, for their lack of investment in jungle rope bridges. The good/clever ones in the audience are praised because they not only get the call backs, but also enter into an imaginative universe where they pretend to remember the 1980s under Thatcher, when all the jungle rope bridges eventually disappeared: "Thatcher Thatcher Thatcher, jungle rope bridge snatcher!!" To round off the anti-comedy, Lee turns against the joke to reminisce about how in 1986 he and Richard Herring drew up a list of the subjects it was too clichéd to cover that included *Scooby Doo* routines and Thatcher, lamenting: "You grow up to become the things you hate."

The theme of lost hopes and possibilities is recurrent in Lee's work, not least as much of his on stage persona is premised on being "a 90s Comedian", who most people have forgotten or suspect is really someone else (e.g. "Terry Christian has let himself go", etc.). But the subversion is 'used' to identify a gap in the presentation of ourselves within market society. In the final crescendo of 'If You'd Prefer a Milder Comedian Please Ask for One', Lee (2010) remarks on childhood events where he found out about the death of a family member, or that he was adopted. He says how his family would tell him the news with the phrase: "I'll give it to you straight like a pear cider made from 100% pears." The revelation is repeated several times through his grandad, who bombed Dresden, and who never spoke about the war except this one time when Stewart asked and he replied: "I'll give it to you straight like a pear cider made from 100% pears. It was awful what happened, terrible what we did to them." His wife intervenes, "It wasn't as bad as what they did to Coventry." His Grandad replies: "Shut up you don't know what you're talking about." And Lee extends this revelation to a form of 'folk history', that uses the phrase to chart the movement of his family from the rural to the urban centres, and how the upheaval of British working-class history, was mediated by retaining certain cultural idioms.

The gravity of this history is the reason why Lee experienced "such sadness" when he came across an advert, where a chirpy Welsh lad walks into a pub and asks for a pint of Magners with the phrase "give it to me straight like a pear cider made from 100% pears". At this point Lee drops the mic and begins to shout, nearly in tears, asking whether he is expected to believe that they just happened to come up with that phrase? He runs into the audience, and then up the stairs, claiming that he now can't use the phrase cos they've stolen it, how he was gonna teach it to his son, but now he can't. They take everything: people's memories, songs, and beliefs. The subversion is to ridicule the invention of history in advertising, by inventing a history and hating them for the theft. The very possibility of meaning has been re-phrased in the terms of a sentimental market subject.

In a *Guardian* article, he develops this critique of the market subject through a subversion of the use of the Angel of the North to advertise a Morrison's baguette (Lee, 2014b). In the piece, he also raises the issue of Paddy Power drawing a jockey on the 3,000-year-old White Horse of Uffington, remarking:

> If we can advertise on ancient hill figures, and publicise on public art, I wondered, as I drove home across Wales, what other monetisable spaces, previously considered sacred, are we failing to optimise? And then it struck me. The subconscious itself is going to waste. What of those unmanageable moments, where we are struck by beauty and meaning we had not foreseen? They are what makes us human, admittedly, but is there some way to make them pay?
>
> Aiming to cross the Severn by the M4, I stopped at Tintern Abbey, and dragged our sleeping children into the sunlight. Normally I would have pointed them at the romantic ruin and lectured them on how it inspired in Wordsworth, Turner and Tennyson the apprehension of the sublime. Instead, I forcibly marched them around the site, chanting: 'Buy Morrisons bread! Gamble at Paddy Power! Buy Morrisons bread! Gamble at Paddy Power!' until, crying and ashamed, they begged me to stop.
>
> Dovetailing through Caerleon, where the Welsh mystic Arthur Machen saw the Great God Pan, I wandered the woodland glades shouting at walkers, 'Buy Morrisons bread! Gamble at Paddy Power! Buy Morrisons bread! Gamble at Paddy Power!' and then, somewhat distressed, I vomited in the churchyard of St Cadoc's, the residue forming the perfect outline of a Morrisons baguette upon an ancient grave.
>
> We drove on, to the Aust service station on the M4, where, just short of the Severn Bridge, a Vauxhall Cavalier, belonging to Richey Edwards from the Manic Street

Preachers, was found abandoned in February 1995. In the Costa Coffee I carved into my arm with a razor blade the words 'Buy Morrisons bread! Gamble at Paddy Power!' Now no one could doubt my sincerity, my fitness for purpose in this brave new age. My arm hurts. My children are embarrassed. There is sick everywhere. And blood. Who do I invoice? There must be some way of getting all this thoughts and feelings shit to pay for itself? Come on!

3 Satirical literacy

Drawing these arguments together, the rise of radical comedy has made a significant contribution to the substance of everyday comic resistance. Indeed, the previous sections contemplated how radical comedy was an everyday 'theorization' of global political possibility: that the performance of comedy might politicize subjectivity as emotional, hopeful, or even futile. Beyond overpowering renditions of disciplinary or hegemonic power in critical thought, I argue that radical comedy has turned to the specific details of how 'the system' works, through media narratives, through overlapping rationalities of public perception, and the emotive and absurd theatrics of global crisis. Importantly, the substance of radical comedy suggests an unstable, limited, yet highly engaging way of thinking about – *and through* – market subjectivity. A capacity to address and involve the audience in the critique of global politics marks an important movement beyond the open-ended – and ambiguous – practices of irony.

On some level, the question of ethical responsibility, which had appeared merely circumstantial for irony, became a driving force. In the work of Brooker, Brand and Lee, comic resistances re-phrase the everyday market subject as a vital category, in a manner that carries affective power, helping us to question how global politics is entwined with – indeed *known through* – emotion. This ability to draw together – and subvert – apparently separate issues, such as between the state form of democracy and Paxman's role as an emotional subject, gives radical comedy an interesting reflexive quality. Engaging the affective dimension(s) of market subjectivity, through the identification of suffering, boredom and anger (which both perpetuate and resist dominant rationalities), gets to the lived experiences of everyday market life in a way that can anticipate new modes of subjectification.

In the work of Russell Brand, this affective depth encourages reflection on alternative political narratives, awareness raising for socialism and spirituality, such that the 'involving' and vital dimensions of resistance might open up new vistas for political engagement. For Brooker, the subject of austerity is increasingly 'produced' as a hating being, his comic resistance invites reflection on how market government is achieved. For Lee, anger at the self, becomes the only possible way of sustaining a critical reflexivity through the dilemma of meaning and markets. Echoing some of Iannucci's work, Lee's comedy generates a more tragic reflection, that there might 'not' be correct ways forward for resistance; that the subject is so intimately entwined with market rationalities, all we can hope for is some absurd sense of awareness:

> 'Did you see Stewart Lee?' 'Yeh.' 'Was it funny?' 'No. *But I agreed the fuck out of it!*'... [pause] ... I'm not interested in laughs. What I'm aiming for is a temporary mass liberal consensus ... that dissolves on contact with air. (Lee, 2014c)

Despite these important contributions to the theory and practice of everyday resistance, however, it is nevertheless possible to discern important ambiguities and limits in the radical turn. Instrumentally, questions can be asked about the achievement of a radical form of politics that recommends 'against' voting. More critically, we might wonder about the positionality of these reflexive and heroic male comedians. Once again, the protagonists of British comedy are all white males, occupying an increasingly privileged position within (mediatized) society. Apologies might be made of course. For all that Russell Brand's celebrity star rose through his anti-establishment position, it is important not to understate the role of his appeal in making a genuine difference to the profile (and eventual success) of campaigns like the Focus E15 campaign by single mothers. Equally, the lack of diversity in British comedy is something that Stewart Lee has addressed directly in his Alternative Comedy Experience, which dedicates itself to profiling and interviewing new or marginal talents like Josie Long, and highlighting the difficulty of making it in the hierarchical and elitist British comedy industry. But such apologia would miss the point.

On the argument of this book, resistance does not somehow step outside of power, or 'overcome' it in some way. That comedians occupy a place within power is not a de-legitimation of resistance, so much as a signal of the ethical responsibility involved. In this vein, Brand and Brooker demonstrate alternative modes (and sites) of political engagement; through networks, through the internet, and even snark.

For Brand, his star value was a strategic attention booster for anti-austerity protests – even *Sky News* ran a special section on him taking his shirt off (?!). More productively, his *Trews* video demonstrated the possibilities of embracing the new media forms available through social media, something that has gradually taken hold in UK political activism on both the left and he right, for example, Novara Media and UnHerd. Equally, a range of new techniques of the political are mooted by Brooker, who provides a strong example of how to inhabit the media-market nexus in an empowering manner.

Indeed, Brooker has been consistently impressive for his ability to weave together snark with deeper intellectual critiques of the postmodern malaise, especially through the inclusion of short documentary sections by Adam Curtis, which introduce concepts like individualization and non-linear warfare to a broad comedy audience. While there is no necessary association between this kind of work and wider practices of resistance, it is clear that Brooker, in particular, is able to embody a vital image of this mode of political engagement. Examples of how this kind of thinking can prefigure new forms of resistance might include the proliferation of political satire through social networks, for example the *Daily Mash*? Or else, it might be seen in line with a wider vernacular of commodity-oriented resistance such as *Brandalism* or other forms of consumer subversion?[14] Such lines of thought/action are attractive precisely because they allow everyday market subjects a novel route into the politics of their subjectivation.

On this view, resistance to market subjectivity is performative of new modes of market life. Satirical performances are not closed events; they are received and reiterated, modified and subverted. Against an instrumental concern with the 'political impact' of satire, I argue we should also explore the proliferation of satire as an everyday language of political life. As Stephen Wagg (2002: 324) argues: 'satire has become deeply woven into public discourse and has helped to define a new paradigm for the mediation of the public sphere'. Yet, while this theme has been reflected in previous chapters, I would argue that the rise of radical comedy, especially in terms of its direct call to arms for everyday market subjects, perpetuates a more profound dilemma.

What happens when satirical literacy is generalized as a form of radical political engagement in the public sphere of global politics? Archetypically, by providing such a robust critique of politics, Iannucci has arguably created an alternative critical register for thinking

---

14 http://brandalism.ch/

about – and practising – British political life. Through its popularity, *The Thick of It* fostered a kind of satirical literacy about Spin Doctors and Spads, about gesture politics and public relations. The now popular refrain that one or other political event is 'just like an episode of *The Thick of It*' suggests a reflexive language of engagement. For example, Jeremy Corbyn's reference to "ordinary people doing extraordinary things" in his speech to the Annual Labour Party Conference (Corbyn, 2015), which was word-for-word what Nicola Murray says about "Fourth Sector Pathfinders", was noted by Iannucci himself (*Evening Standard*, 2015). Equally, the rise of social media parody accounts has regularly and commonly referenced the programme: for example, the Twitter account of Peter Mannion MP parodied the early Brexit brainstorming sessions as a version of the 'ideas retreat' in Series 3, with Mannion asking 'Am I Norway-Plus'? These are not issues of political impact, but they do suggest a productive dimension to satirical performance, where the terms of engagement are updated, generalized and modified.

While comedy fans may 'enjoy' this extension, whereby politics itself becomes a form of satire, it is clear that we are in unstable territory. Beyond the positive image of satirical literacy, we may also need to consider the role of politics and media in the recuperation of critique. What happens, for instance, when politicians appear in a satirical light? Remarking upon the use of his jokes by David Cameron, Iannucci (2016) suggested that one reason not to turn the joke back against him is that 'politicians no longer act like real versions of themselves. Instead, they come over as replicants of an idealised, fictional version of what they think a politician should be. They perform politics, rather than practise policy. [...] We're left watching an entertainment rather than participating in affairs of state.' On these terms, Stewart Lee (2014a) has referred to (the invented character of) Boris Johnson as the 'world's first self-satirising politician'.

Importantly though, the everyday merging between satire and politics does not seem to turn people off from politics, indeed, it might be argued that one reason for the massive public engagement in the European Union referendum was precisely the irreverent style of 'self-satirising' politicians like Boris and Nigel Farage. More critically, though, it does challenge us to find new modes of intervention. In this vein, Charlie Brooker offers the most direct reflection on the question of how to engage in global politics. His deconstruction of media narratives, decentring of the viewer subject, and his use of an open-ended performance where viewer subjects are invited to reflect on their own positionality, arguably leaves the 'work' of politics to the audience.

Satirical engagement can be both unpredictable and uncoordinated, as David Cameron found with the 'PigGate' allegation, which became a social media meme reflexive to the eerie parallels with Charlie Brooker's *Black Mirror* episode 'The National Anthem'. Can the rise of satirical literacy form a productive backdrop for such engagement? Rebecca Higgie (2017) describes a form of 'citizen satire', how ordinary people engage critically with politics via social media memes, as a significant proliferation of agency. While the potentials of a bottom-up form of public sphere populated by citizen satirists should not be romanticized, it is clear that new moral economies of satire are emerging on social media that are quickly circulated and highly inclusive. They may be rough around the edges, encourage a form of attack-level politics, or even take on a conspiratorial tone, but as an everyday form of politics, the growth of citizen satire does not so much diminish but rather *changes the terms of* political engagement.

Conclusion

This chapter has analysed a distinctively radical turn in British comedy that focused on the logics and rationalities of 'the system' to question the performance and subversion of everyday subjects. While aspects of radical comedy may be associated with a suffocating effect, whereby all forms of intervention are rendered meaningless in the face of such overwhelming power structures, I have traced a more empowering line. In particular, the democratic engagements of Brand and the recovery of the contingency of agency in Brooker and Lee, was an important shift in satirical understandings of the site and nature of global politics. Again, the implications and unintended consequences of this shift are challenging. Radical comedy contributed to a widespread anti-establishment and anti-elite sentiment that dovetailed with the rise of social media and hashtag politics in the same period. This generalization of satirical literacy was productive of new modes of deliberation that would have profound consequences for the nature and form of global political engagement.

6

Brexit, or How I Learned
to Stop Worrying and Love
the Single Market

Introduction: Politicizing comedy

British comedy emerged in relation to some important political questions, imperial decline, deregulation, globalization and, more reflexively, the ethical ambiguities entailed in comedy itself, for example, over class, race, gender and so on. On this view, comedy is an everyday vernacular of resistance through which global politics is known, legitimated and contested. Less a tool, than a space of politics in its own right. Indeed, the previous chapter argued that radical comedy foregrounded a politics of agency within the (affective) context of global market life. While potentially more engaging (and responsible) than the ironic form that preceded it, the popularity of radical comedy also created its own limits, of race, gender and 'celebrity'. Indeed, it arguably commodified a type of anti-austerity critique that increasingly manifested in the public sphere. Suddenly, the 'anti-establishment' anger of radical comedy was celebrated – *and facilitated* – by social media platforms, satirical memes and hashtag politics. We are all satirists now.

If British comedy is an important and productive element in the politics of globalization, then it might have been expected to play a pivotal role in the politics of Brexit. The famously unexpected British vote to leave the European Union (EU) was widely seen as a challenge to cultural values of social inclusion and progress, values that arguably resonate with (the self-identity of) British comedy. Yet, for many, the actual experience of comedy after Brexit has been a disappointing failure. On the one hand, the instrumental critique looms large, that, despite an overwhelming comic turn against Brexit, rather obviously, the plethora of anti-Brexit jokes did not manage to affect the result of the referendum. On the other hand, more critically, the routine practice of joking about the 'folly' of Brexit, the 'stupidity' of its leaders, as well as the commonly referenced 'ignorance' and 'racism' of 'the Leave voter', rather had the effect of entrenching division.

In this way, the global event of Brexit saw profound challenges levelled 'at' comedy itself. For so long the bastion of liberal left resistance, the vote to leave the EU set off a period of palpable disquiet over the substance and political value of comedy and satire. There was a veritable outpouring of instrumental critique in the public sphere. Comedians like Russell Brand were criticized for telling people 'not' to vote, while 'comedy politicians' like Boris Johnson and Nigel Farage were castigated for their use of humour to manipulate voters. Had comedy failed? Was the rise of radical comedy just another successful commodity that distracted us from the insidious effects of irony in public life? Did Armando Iannucci cause Brexit?

Against such popular lines of critique, this chapter will argue that the very attempt to 'police' comedy for its role in Brexit can reveal important insights about the everyday politics of globalization. In this vein, it is important to address a pervasive argument among pro-Brexit commentators, which suggested that 'liberal comedians' had disavowed their resistant identities by so thoroughly endorsing Remain. Far from a failure of comedy, this position suggests that the protracted debates and contests that typified Brexit politics demonstrate an all-too-comfortable relationship between comedy and 'the establishment'. Rather than choose between 'sides' in this debate, this chapter seeks to question what is produced: what emerges when we figure comedy as a key a site of (intense) political divides? My aim is to re-phrase the comedy of Brexit in terms of a socially consequential practice that teases at the (changing) social and political consensus. Against those who might discern in Brexit a thoroughly divisive tragedy, I will explore how comedy can be an adaptive language, capable of reflecting (on) its own positionality, while allowing for fundamental conflicts and disagreements to play out. Comedy as politics.

Section 1 introduces the discussion by addressing two of the prevailing critiques of comedy after Brexit. Initial reactions to the Brexit vote identified a special new form of 'joker politician' in the guise of Boris Johnson and Nigel Farage, who had 'hoodwinked' the population with their 'oafish wit' and 'irreverent barbs'. In the context of crisis, this instrumental critique sought to stabilize a division between (silly) comedy and (serious) politics. There was a typical lament for the 'good old days' of proper satire that 'punched up' in the name of 'progressive politics'. Against this view, a range of comedians and commentators articulated a more critical idea of the 'comedy establishment'. Indeed, they noted the near universal prevalence of anti-Brexit comedy as a sign that British comedy was no longer resistant, but merely a legitimating figure *within* the EU liberal market consensus. While this formed a focal point for pro-Leave arguments about a wider 'cultural conspiracy' to Remain, the debate nevertheless provokes an interesting set of questions about the political role and positionality of the professional comedian. Indeed, it (partly) echoes previous critiques of the recuperation of irony within the prevailing consensus of commodity culture.

Section 2 will question how post-Brexit comedy has evolved to embrace the 'culture wars'. This has been especially true on the libertarian/right wing of comedy, where a long tradition of irony over political correctness has been taken up by comedians like Jonathan Pie as well as satirical characters like Godfrey Elfwick and Titania McGrath. On the one hand, such comedy goes to the heart of the dominant value systems of neoliberal capitalism, asking about how far ideals of political correctness, inclusivity and 'hate speech' have become corrosive in a public sphere, which can sometimes seem like it is structured around a permanent politics of offence. On the other hand, their 'argument' that the daily outrage of social media is part of a coherent liberal hegemony is somewhat disingenuous. While the intellectual point (and joke) is coherent, their practice of trolling and baiting is *symptomatic*, rather than subversive of the problem they identify.

Finally, section 3 will question whether and how comedy might be 'moving on' from the divisive politics of Brexit, to embrace a more plural tone. Here the polyphonic nature of anti-Brexit comedy has moved to focus on the elites who supported it, rather than stereotypes of the people who voted for it. For example, *The Mash Report* has regularly featured the pro-Brexit comedian Geoff Norcott, and there is a growing mainstream acceptability for 'right-wing' comedy. This mood change is further embodied *and subverted* in the work of Stewart Lee (2018a), and discussion will reflect on a letter he wrote to fans that asked where his comedy could credibly go after Brexit had dissolved 'the cultural consensus' that shaped his comedy.

1 Brexit and the division of British comedy

The vote to leave the EU provoked a number of satirical responses, many of which were critical of Brexit, and fewer that were positive. Despite apparent division, however, this section will attempt to move beyond a vision of comedy as a simple case of 'joking for our side'. Of course, such jokes were keenly embraced after Brexit, as per descriptions of Nigel Farage as a 'frog faced arse wipe' on *The Last Leg*, or the hilarity that ensued when Danny Dyer repeatedly called David Cameron a 'Twat' on *Good Evening Britain*. However, I will argue the intensity of post-Brexit politics has also fermented opportunities for professional comedians to innovate. On one level, it is quite hard to tour an anti-Brexit comedy show when the audiences that a comedian encounters might be Remain, Leave, or 50:50. Indeed, Marcus Brigstocke famously recounted how Brexit forced him to re-think his comedy in light of audience walk-outs (Sillito, 2017). On another level, the intense political scrutiny of comedy has forced some genuine reflections on what it means to be resistant after Brexit. While the easy association of comedy with 'the left' has always been problematic, the preponderance of Remain supporting comedians has brought that idea into sharp relief. Simply put, making jokes about ignorant working-class Leave voters is not a great look if you claim to be anti-establishment. This section will therefore attempt to map out the various elements and limits to this apparent divide within British comedy by engaging two significant discourses: the *comedy politician* and the *comedy establishment*.

The comedy politician

> 'When you look at the EU now, it reminds me, it makes me think of ... walking round this wonderful underwear factory, it makes me think of some badly designed undergarment that has now become too tight in some places, far too tight, far too constrictive, and *dangerously loose* in other places.'[1]

A prominent early discourse on comedy and Brexit centred on the instrumental argument that one reason why Leave had won was that the campaign was fronted by politicians who had a special facility for humour. While this discourse was ostensibly orchestrated around the body of the politician, especially Johnson and Farage, it also contemplated a wider set of issues about the role of comedy and satire in politics. This discourse is important, therefore, because it establishes a framework for regulating comedy and comedians as 'separate' from

---

[1]   Boris Johnson speech during Leave campaign, 16 May 2016, https://www.youtube.com/watch?v=N-5YcGT2iV8 (accessed 27 July 2018).

politics, a separation that I will argue is both unstable and prone to failure. This might be because comedy is inherently political, or that politics – especially Brexit politics – is inherently comic (Weaver, 2019). Moreover, as previous chapters have argued, it is also because the relationship between comedy and politics is contingently emergent through discursive performances, receptions and subversions. As such, the debate is constitutive of certain possibilities and limits that are both emergent and contested by comedians themselves.

The discourse of the 'comedy politician' centred on two overlapping arguments which circulated in the wake of the Brexit vote. The first was that politicians like Boris Johnson and Nigel Farage were either buffoons, or they had cynically used their 'clown-like' personas to disguise the 'reality' of their (neoliberal and/or racist) politics. The second argument was extrapolated to cover the wider – often negative – ramifications of this mixing between comedy and politics. The overriding tone of this discourse was a lament for a time when 'proper comedy' was handled by skilled professional satirists who sought to hold politicians to account. While politicians were presumed to have a seriousness of purpose and facility for fair judgement. Instead, what many critics now saw was an unedifying mix of politics and 'entertainment' that lacked credibility and justified, for many, the 'national humiliation' of Brexit as a host of international publications invoked various *Monty Python* sketches to represent the 'self-harm' of that the UK was inflicting on itself.[2]

In visual terms, the discourse of comedy politicians is easily performed via images of Boris stuck on a zip wire, waving union jack flags, or Boris wiping out a Japanese school child in a rugby match. Several such images came together to present the idea of 'clownish' politicians who were an embarrassment to themselves and the nation. While Farage does not play on precisely the same 'oafish charm' as Boris, there was nevertheless scope to work with his 'frog-like' face and 'unflinching' confidence. Appearing on *Question Time*, Russell Brand, in particular, questioned the amiable and humorous way in which the media image of Nigel Farage is relayed:

---

[2] Quintessentially, *The New Yorker* ran with a cover page of some men from the *Ministry of Silly Walks* stepping over a cliff edge. This line has been repeated regularly in critical discourses on Brexit, increasingly by EU politicians who commonly reference the 'Black Knight' scene, where a knight doesn't know when to stop fighting.

'As much as any of us I enjoy seeing Nigel Farage in a boozer with a pint and a fag laughing off his latest scandals about breastfeeding or whatever, I enjoy it.... But this man is not a cartoon character. He ain't Del Boy. He ain't Arthur Daley. He is a pound shop Enoch Powell, and we've got to watch him.'[3]

In this way, there was greater depth and nuance to the discourse of the comedy politician than a simple sneer at the ridiculous buffoons who had caused Brexit. After all, if they were really so silly, how could they have possibly 'caused' Brexit? An important line in the argument was developed in an article by Jonathan Coe (2013) that the *London Review of Books* began circulating on the day of the Brexit vote.

In the article, entitled: 'Sinking Giggling into the Sea', Coe used his review of a book – *The Wit and Wisdom of Boris Johnson* – to develop a critique of the role of satire in politics. Taking a lead from the satire boom of the 1960s, Coe argues that the spirit of satire is 'anti-establishment'; the themes that concerned *Beyond the Fringe* were the church, the judiciary, the government. However, as the popularity of satire grew, its facility for producing laughter must be questioned, first gently, on the grounds that the main exponents emerge from the androcentric, upper-class, Oxbridge educated circles that make up the establishment, and then critically, because the commodification of comedy creates little more than a product to be consumed. In this way, Coe positions the career of Boris Johnson in terms of his appearances on *Have I Got News For You* and the way he was able to play the role of the 'nasty Tory' politician *for laughs* because: 'he understands that the laughter it generates, correctly harnessed, can be very useful to a politician who knows what to do with it'. On this view, the cutting edge of satire has been blunted as the clown politician has entered into a symbiotic relationship with comedy:

In an age when politicians are judged first of all on personality, when the public assumes all of them to be deceitful, and when it's easier and much more pleasurable to laugh about a political issue than to think about it, Johnson's apparent self-deprecating honesty and lack of concern for his own dignity were bound to make him a hit. (Coe, 2013)

---

[3] Russell Brand and Nigel Farage on *Question Time*, 11 December 2014, https://www.youtube.com/watch?v=R7i-JIw1zig (accessed 11 May 2020).

This view of Johnson proved very popular in the period after the Brexit vote. It provided a critical heuristic for thinking through how the Leave campaign had *disguised* their message. As Coe (2013) argued, 'If we are chuckling at him, we are not likely to be thinking too hard about his doggedly neoliberal and pro-City agenda, let alone doing anything to counter it.' On this view, if he was eating a Cornish pasty in Cornwall, or joking in an underwear factory ('Knickers to the pessimists!'), then the people were unlikely to be thinking too hard about the *real politics* of Leave. Indeed, similar points were echoed by Will Davies (2016), who suggested that far from contesting politics, satire had now become a servant of Leave politicians:

> 'The willingness of Nigel Farage to weather the scornful laughter of metropolitan liberals (for instance through his periodic appearances on *Have I Got News For You*) could equally have made him look brave in the eyes of many potential Leave voters. I can't help feeling that every smug, liberal, snobbish barb that Ian Hislop threw his way on that increasingly hateful programme was ensuring that revenge would be all the greater, once it arrived. The giggling, from which Boris Johnson also benefited handsomely, needs to stop.'

On both accounts, the discourse of the comedy politician presents a sophisticated hybrid, someone who has learned that – in the absence of trust in politicians – it is possible to laugh at themselves in order to take ownership of the problem. In this way, comedy becomes an element in statecraft, and the politician curates a comic persona. Johnson crafts an 'anti-establishment', renegade, bumbling image of himself that both performs and subverts the Etonian elite stereotype of a Tory. Likewise, Farage is able to chuckle away 'outside' the elite, down the pub with the real people. Indeed, the crafted 'man in the street' persona is a neat trick for someone who went to public school and worked in finance. Moreover, as Brand identified, Farage has also played on his 'everyman' qualities to conjure a kind of irreverence towards the EU (and the Tory party) that arguably references older tropes of comedy as 'cheeky' and 'rude'. In one of his 'final' speeches to the EU Parliament he mused over how MEPs used to laugh at him when he first arrived, concluding triumphantly: *'you're not laughing now are you!'*[4]

---

[4] ' "You're not laughing at me now" – Farage tells MEPs', 28 June 2016, https://www.youtube.com/watch?v=fNS5dQbun4s (accessed 11 May 2020).

Two weeks after this address, a short video began to circulate on social media. Farage spoke in front of an MP who seemed to gesture – in universal fashion – that Farage was a 'wanker'. The video circulated with gleeful re-tweets and replies that someone was finally being honest about Farage. It was suggested that the video crystallized the mood of a nation, with many commentators expressing dismay that Farage portrays himself as the voice of the UK in Europe, when he can't even get elected back home. However, what looked set to become a viral sensation, was quickly questioned in the comments section. The apparent hero with the hand gesture turned out to be Ray Finch, a fellow member of UKIP, and a counter-view began to circulate that the true subject of the accusation was in fact Juncker. Suddenly the mood in the comments sections turned to scorn as people began to comment that this was precisely the kind of abusive and childish politics that had brought such shame on our nation.[5]

The comedy establishment

The 'comedy politician' discourse attempts to separate out comedy and politics in order to stabilize the latter. While politicians have always used humour as a form of statecraft – indeed, when many in the public sphere support the use of satirical memes by, *inter alia*, Corbyn's Labour, Donald Tusk and Emmanuel Macron (Dean, 2019) – there has been a significant repudiation of right-wing/Leave politicians' use of humour. The use of comedy by Johnson and Farage is taken to imply bad faith, that they cannot be trusted. However, with a divisive subject like Brexit, a second discourse on comedy and politics emerged that came from 'the Right'. A number of Leave-supporting commentators and comedians identified a dissonance between their 'victory' in the referendum and the widespread cultural performance of Leave voters as 'idiots' and 'racists'. If the 'comedy politician' discourse had noted the links between comedians and the upper echelons of British society as 'a qualification' on the resistant potential of satire, then the 'comedy establishment' discourse weaponized this view. Far from being seen as a resistant force, 'liberal comedy' would now be implicated in the hegemonic common sense of an EU capitalist hierarchy that was in the midst of a fundamental social 'revolt'.

---

[5]   While many of the tweets were subsequently deleted, the initial story still received some minor press coverage. See https://www.her.ie/lol/this-politician-taking-the-mick-out-of-nigel-farage-is-doing-what-were-all-think-300407 (accessed 11 May 2020).

The 'comedy establishment' discourse emerged from two overlapping arguments that both carried a reactionary quality, pushing back against the mood of negativity that seemed to engulf the UK after the Brexit vote. First, those promoting the idea of a 'cultural conspiracy' to subvert the Leave vote began to identify the role of media and metropolitan elites in refusing to accept the result of the referendum. A critical extension of this view suggested that professional comedians held an 'all-too-comfortable' position in the EU liberal market consensus; that 'liberal comedy' had become hegemonic, and jokes now had to be judged in terms of whether or not they portrayed the 'right kind of political opinion' (read: cosmopolitan, pro-European and diversity-promoting). Second, a critical variant of the 'political correctness gone mad' agenda developed a related critique of the liberal values of the comedy establishment as a new form of cultural discipline. Simply put, was anti-Brexit comedy guilty of the very problems of racism, misogyny and – most fundamentally – *hatred of the working classes* that it claimed to question?

In material terms the 'comedy establishment' discourse was easily represented in terms of wealth, mainstream media presence (especially BBC), and the palpable fact that almost 100% of comedians were pro-Remain. Especially in the UK, where comedy is taken very seriously as part of the national culture, this linking of satire to elitism was a powerful discourse, not least because of the apparent connections between British comedy and left-wing resistance. If comedy really was such an 'open' and pluralist discourse, why was there only one openly Tory, pro-Brexit comedian at the 2016 Edinburgh festival? Brendan O'Neill (2017) summarized the position in a typically 'provocative' piece for *The Spectator*:

> Britain's comics are almost universally anti-Brexit. The conformism is staggering. [...] that a hulking swathe of the populace rejects the EU, but hardly a single comic does, shows how utterly disconnected the comic class really is. It confirms the colonisation of British comedy by a breathtakingly narrow stratum of society.

By using references to a 'comic class' and ideas about the 'colonisation' of comedy, the discourse suggests that conformity of opinion emerges from a hegemonic position within – *and for* – power. The 'comedy establishment' emerges as a critical discourse that portrays Brexit as a rebellion by the 'lower orders'. Instead, for O'Neill, the 'comic class' is 'being overrun by well-fed toffs or well-connected middle classes who tend to share the same world view. Hence the cultural elite now thinks one thing and ordinary people think another.'

While it might be argued that 'not all comedians' are rich and successful, or that 'not all comedians' are blind to the range of different reasons why people voted to leave, there is no doubt that the idea of the 'comedy establishment' had impact. At one level, a number of comedians reflected on the difficulty of doing anti-Brexit comedy. In particular, Marcus Brigstocke went public with his concerns, indeed his doubt and uncertainty, about how to deal with such a divisive topic as Brexit (Sillito, 2017). While comfortably anti-Brexit in his comedy, Brigstocke reflected upon how uncomfortable he felt about repeated audience walk-outs during his live shows: 'People have been angry; people have walked out of shows and people have booed. A lot of the people that I think of as my audience will not be back – they won't come again – they're that angry.' At another level, comedians and comedy writers began to question the nature of anti-Brexit comedy. Was it really funny? Aaron Brown, editor of the British Comedy Guide website, argued that Brexit comedy was 'exclusively negative.... Many jokes essentially paraphrase [it] as *shooting ourselves in the foot*, and the rest rely on lazily branding 52 per cent of the voters as racist' (see Sabur, 2017) On this view, Brown (quoted in Sabur, 2017) mentioned the idea of a dynamic interaction between comedians and their audiences:

> One would have hoped comedians would be able to find comic mileage in their evident disengagement from half of the public, but there instead seems to be little to no such acceptance and analysis of the referendum result, instead merely anger and lashing out at stupid people making the wrong decision, as they see it. As far as audience reaction goes, it tends to be fairly warm with television studio audiences as most such recordings take place in the resolutely pro-remain London, but in the rest of the country – England and Wales, at very least – one can only begin to imagine how alienated and offended some audiences must feel.

Against the bad faith image of comedy in relation to Brexit then, the 'comedy establishment' discourse invites a different, albeit potentially totalizing vision, that 'liberal comedians' are a part of the ideological superstructure of EU capitalism. When faced with a challenge to their hegemony, the 'comic class' has actually turned against the working classes they purport to sympathize with. As the pro-Brexit comedian Geoff Norcott put it:

> 'normally in political satire, it's a case of attacking the ideas, or the Party. You play the ball not the man, but this was the other way round, one of the first satirical responses to Brexit was to call everyone stupid and racist, so there was that sort "peephole moment", where you go "oh right, it's like that is it?"'

And particularly when a lot of the people who voted Leave were working-class people. It came from the left, who often prize the idea of "punching up", but now they were "punching down" (Norcott, 2018a). More critically, in one of his stand-up shows, Norcott openly questioned the balance of racist attitudes on the Remain side:

> 'Brexit. Telling me I'm a fucking racist cos I voted Leave, right ... working-class people are on the fucking frontline of racial integration. Do you know what I mean? *We've actually got friends* in those communities! Our kids might even be in classes with those people, they might come over for tea, our kids might date people from that community. Don't fucking tell me about racism when all it comes down to is artisan bread, fuck you! [Posh accent] "Well I mean you know, who's gonna come and pick the strawberries or work at Pret?" Wow I didn't know that was what the EU was there for, just to provide you with economic oompa loompas, eh? Maybe you'll actually have to pay the going rate for childcare?' (Norcott, 2018b)

On this view, the class, racial and gender politics of Remain voters is foregrounded in a way that 'might' reflect a more sophisticated take on the politics of Brexit than 'cosmopolitan Remainers' vs. 'racist Leavers'? Possibly, or possibly not, given the move to stereotype Remainers. Far more likely, I would suggest, is the continuation of an impasse over the very terms of (comic) debate.

2 Embracing the culture wars?

While the 'comedy politician' and 'comedy establishment' discourses do much to illustrate how jokes are far more political than might be supposed, it is clear that they don't necessarily take us beyond the divisive politics of Brexit. Indeed, they could just as easily be portrayed as two fundamentally opposed cultural imaginaries that emerge from – and reproduce – the divisive politics of Brexit; akin to the way pro-Remain *and* pro-Leave voters were equally prone to regard the BBC as biased towards the other side. Whereas the first discourse seeks to stabilize politics and return comedy to its role as a 'healthy purveyor of scepticism' in public life, the second portrays that very ideal of comedy as painfully naïve about the nature of cultural hierarchies in capitalist society. Against the caricature of cynical clowns in government, they provide a caricature of propertied elites concerned about the maintenance of supply chains for their avocado toast.

This section will now examine the emergence of a new strain in British comedy that arguably follows in the tradition of irony over political correctness identified in Chapter 4, but which updates the approach to address what it regards as the specific – *and specifically ridiculous* – politics of a post-Brexit, post-truth politics. This movement is particularly interesting because it breaks with the idea that comic resistance must portray a specifically left-wing politics. Indeed, partly as a result, a number of the protagonists have themselves been critiqued as racist and fascist. What is perhaps most interesting about this new form of satire, however, is the way it engages with the divisions of post-truth politics – not from a pro- or anti-Brexit standpoint, but through a direct subversion of the values of liberalism – which have been so animated in relation to the EU. Moreover, the form of the humour has directly inhabited the techniques and technologies of post-truth: viral videos and internet trolling. In particular, Jonathan Pie has developed a form of humour that attempts to satirize both left and right, pro- and anti-Brexit, as well as the 'liberal hegemony' of woke.

An early precursor to this challenging form of humour can be found in the work of the proto-alt-right satire of *Godfrey Elfwick*, an anonymous Twitter persona focused on the subversion of mainstream liberal multicultural sensibilities. Self-described as a 'Genderqueer Muslim atheist. Born white in the #wrongskin', Godfrey Elfwick set out to portray an extreme version of what the alt-right deride as social justice warriors. In short, his Twitter feed attempts to filter all of "life through the lens of minority issues". On one level, Elfwick clearly echoes the kind of humour portrayed in Gervais' *Equality Street*, his own pinned tweet reading: "Imagine being so ignorant that you'd ignore a person's gender, ethnicity, or sexual preference and just treat them the same as everyone else." On another level though, the nature of his trolling arguably takes the potentials of alt-right satire in a new direction. In one early 'score', he managed to get interviewed on the BBC talking about the racial discrimination of *Star Wars* – "The main bad guy – what's he called, Dark Raider? – is black, he has a deep voice, he listens to rap music – it's just a really bad racial stereotype." In this sense, Elfwick seeks to let his satire 'play out' in unpredictable ways, which can be both comic and problematic depending on *which side* you favour in the culture wars.

In another, quite famous article for *The Guardian*, that Elfwick claimed to have written: '"Alt-right" online poison nearly turned me into a racist' (Anonymous, 2016), Elfwick charted a story of his online radicalization: 'I voted remain in the referendum. The thought of racism in any form has always been abhorrent to me. When leave won, I was devastated.' In response, he claims that – as a good liberal – he decided to investigate why people voted Leave: 'Surely they were not all racist, bigoted or hateful?'

> I watched some debates on YouTube. Obvious points of concern about terrorism were brought up. A leaver cited Sam Harris as a source. I looked him up: this 'intellectual, free-thinker' was very critical of Islam. Naturally my liberal kneejerk reaction was to be shocked, but I listened to his concerns and some of his debates. This, I think, is where YouTube's 'suggested videos' can lead you down a rabbit hole. Moving on from Harris, I unlocked the Pandora's box of 'It's not racist to criticise Islam!' content. Eventually I was introduced, by YouTube algorithms, to Milo and various 'anti-SJW' videos (SJW, or social justice warrior is a pejorative directed at progressives). […] For three months I watched this stuff grow steadily more fearful of Islam. 'Not Muslims,' they would usually say, 'individual Muslims are fine.' But Islam was presented as a 'threat to western civilisation'. […] At the same time, the anti-SJW stuff also moved on to anti-feminism, men's rights activists – all that stuff. I followed a lot of these people on Twitter, but never shared any of it. I just passively consumed it, because, deep down, I knew I was ashamed of what I was doing. I'd started to roll my eyes when my friends talked about liberal, progressive things. What was wrong with them? Did they not understand what being a *real* liberal was? All my friends were just SJWs. They didn't know that free speech was under threat and that politically correct culture and censorship were the true problem. On one

> occasion I even, I am ashamed to admit, very diplomatically
> expressed negative sentiments on Islam to my wife. Nothing
> 'overtly racist', just some of the 'innocuous' type of things
> the YouTubers had presented: 'Islam isn't compatible with
> western civilisation.' She was taken aback: 'Isn't that a bit
> ... right wing?' I justified it: 'Well, I'm more a left-leaning
> centrist. PC culture has gone too far, we should be able to
> discuss these things without shutting down the conversation
> by calling people racist, or bigots.' *The indoctrination was
> complete.*

The satire in this piece is subtle, he writes as someone who is a good
liberal Remain voter who is trying to 'understand' Leave voters, as
if they were some kind of irrational paradox. Of course, the power
is generated by the fact that *The Guardian* apparently took the
bait: adjudicating that it dealt with issues that were pertinent to the
post-Brexit period. On this view, rather than dismissing Leave voters
as racist and bigoted, they are instead portrayed and performed as an
anthropological subject: *how can we understand their apparent irrationality?*
The answer provided by Elfwick, is that they have been indoctrinated
by social media and YouTube videos, pushed to the (apparently)
unacceptable position that: 'we should be able to discuss these things
without shutting down the conversation by calling people racist, or
bigots'.

Like Chris Morris, this form of satire interacts with the world in order
to generate reactions that miss the irony. Unlike Chris Morris, I would
argue, the joke and the joker is readily woven to 'a position' in the
culture wars. When Elfwick eventually stopped working, partly due to
being banned on Twitter, a number of right-wing commentators sought
to eulogize his work and defend his humour on free speech grounds.
Indeed, comedy writers like Andrew Doyle, adapted the technique for
new characters like Titania McGrath, while *The Spectator* commissioned
a new character, Jarvis Dupont, to write a regular column in the
vein of Godfrey Elfwick. Regardless of the positionality, however,
there is something important afoot in comedy, which licenses a more
confrontational, often libertarian form of comedy that challenges the
(social media) audience to question the everyday moralities of Brexit.

Quintessentially, Jonathan Pie has risen to fame in the post-Brexit
period through a number of viral videos that ridicule the current
period for its surfeit of emotion and divisive logics. The humour is to
portray a news anchor who is caught between recorded news feeds, as
he attempts to comprehend the bizarre and inflated politics of Brexit:

[Recorded Feed] 'And many who are calling for a vote on the final Brexit deal are suggesting that the majority of Leave voters were ill-informed and didn't know what they were voting for …' [Unrecorded Feed] '… and meanwhile I am fucking sick of this fucking bullshit. Sorry Tim, sorry, if we are gonna be saying that Leavers are ill-informed, then please can you prove to me that Remainers aren't? Ok, ask your average Remainer, to explain in detail the relationship between the EU Parliament and the EU Commission. How does that work? Yeh, I'll tell you how it works, badly and undemocratically! Ok, I am a Remainer, but I am fucking sick of this assumption that all Leave voters are thick and ill-informed and probably more than just a little bit racist. It's too fucking easy …'[6]

As is perhaps clear, the language is written in a strong rational form, seeking to build or deconstruct logical positions. For example, in this monologue he builds to an entirely serious suggestion, based on polling data, that people voted Leave because: "they believed that the laws that governed this country should be made in this country. They voted on a principle of sovereignty that doesn't require a nuanced knowledge of how Brussels implements legislation …"[7] The humour of the joke is partly related to the build-up of these logics, as Pie slowly winds himself up to a kind of rage at everything. However, perhaps a more interesting point is that he carefully takes the focus away from judging individuals who voted, in order to return to the elite level politics that moved us to this point:

'the real reason why Brexit is such a shit storm is not because working-class people are thick, or the electorate was woefully ill-informed, it's because the Tories are wilfully prepared to sacrifice all the possible benefits of Brexit to deal with short-term party political problems.'[8]

On this view, Pie arguably channels aspects of alternative and radical comedy – "Brexit is a fucking shit storm because many Tories are using Brexit to position themselves for a power grab when May's premiership

---

[6] 'Breaking News – All leave voters are thick!', 18 June 2018, https://www.youtube.com/watch?v=eEaEBmpu-4o (accessed 11 May 2020).

[7] Ibid.

[8] Ibid.

finally wet farts itself out of existence." But he stops short of 'opposing Brexit' in the way demanded of the other critiques discussed in section 1, instead, suggesting that there might not be an easy way out:

> 'Yes the Tories are bastards, but that doesn't mean the EU aren't. Barnier, Tusk, Juncker, Verhofstadt, these people aren't our friends, these are right-leaning politicians, who are derided in their own country. I'm fucking sick of Brexit. I'm fucking sick of Brexit.'[9]

3 A changing consensus?

Despite the divisive politics of Brexit comedy, this book has argued that humour is a more diverse and ambiguous social practice than simply *joking for our side*. Comedy can do different things in different circumstances. It can be inclusive and empancipatory, yet it can also wound and exclude, through stereotype, humiliation, or simply affirming the values of a particular group. What is sometimes lost in the politics of comedy is how each joke or comedy act is not a 'once and for all' moment of politics. Rather, comedy, as a profession and as a social practice is adaptive over time – an everyday language of political engagement. Attempts to discipline the language, to say that one or other version is correct, or to critique it for its close association with, say, a politician, or the establishment, are simply extensions of politics (which exploit the resonance of comedy with a wider public).

In this final section, therefore, I move beyond the 'either-or' mode of reasoning, to explore a more reflexive capacity in humour, to question positionality and to reflect (upon) political contingency. Instead of seeking to *police* comedy/politics, or contest the starting points of 'legitimate' dialogue, we might embrace the 'rough edges' of post-Brexit humour as part of a changing consensus on politics. In this sense, Jonathan Pie is an interesting moment in post-Brexit comedy because he has emerged through the culture wars, by steadfastly seeking to de-centre and subvert them.[10] However, perhaps the most acute satire of Brexit and its impact on comedy comes from Stewart Lee. Accepting that "this is a very difficult time in history to do stand-up", Stewart Lee (2018a) has developed a routine that reflects deeply on 'his'/'our'

---

[9] Ibid.

[10] Indeed, the BBC commissioned one of his live shows for release, which dealt with satires of both the Tories and the liberal left for its move towards a politics of identity.

own position within the performative politics of Brexit; questioning the role of the comedian in finding a way through this 'dissensus'.

> 'I haven't written any jokes about Brexit, because I was trying to write a show that I could keep on the road for 18 months and as I didn't know how Brexit would pan out I didn't write any jokes about it in case I couldn't use them in the show and monetise the work I've done. I haven't written any jokes about Brexit because I didn't see the point of committing to a course of action for which there's no logical or financial justification. [Crowd laughter and applause] THAT'S RIGHT! Clap the things you agree with! Clap, clap, clap! Agree, agree, agree. "Did you see Stewart Lee in Southend end?" "Yeh." "Was it funny?" "No, but I agreed the fuck out of it. It's almost as if it were targeted at my exact social demographic in a cynical attempt to maintain a future proof audience for long-term mortgage repayment purposes."'

By placing his own position as a market subject within the political economy of (anti-)Brexit comedy, Lee takes ownership of the contingency of humour, questioning its reception within a largely supportive audience (for money). The admission is an important one for his ability to then proceed to what he (or the character of Stewart Lee) "really thinks". He moves through some old-fashioned Tory bashing; that Brexit was the result of the ongoing rivalries of "a small group of competitive posh men". So, "as a student David Cameron put his penis into a dead pig's face" and then to outdo him "Michael Gove put his penis into a *Daily Mail* journalist". At this point, Lee is arguably tripping over the not funny, by focusing on the gendered and bestial othering of public figures, a fact illustrated by his mock childish "Euuuurgggh!" But he qualifies: "caustic wit there like Toby Young, do you like it?" Not only has Lee acknowledged the contingency of his position, but he has exaggerated the vulgarity of the normal anti-Tory schtick to satirize its affinities with the right. The movement allows him to get to the point where he can openly discuss how comedy about Brexit must take place in a fundamentally conflicted context, where he plays to both Remain and Leave audiences:

> 'and the Remain voting cities now, they loom out of the map, don't they, like fantasy citadels, in a Tolkien-esque landscape, wondrous walled cities full of wizards and poets,

and people who can understand data. In the middle of a vast swampy fen, with "here there be trolls" written over it. [mixed laughter] Yeh down here, laughter, up there, people going hang on, "Trolls Stew, that's not a very fair way, you know we are in Leave voting Southend-on-Sea, trolls that's not a very fair way to describe the English and Welsh majority that exercised their democratic right to vote to leave the EU", and it isn't, to be fair.... Look we are gonna leave the EU, that is happening and I think people people have gotta put their differences behind them, and try and make it work. And I don't know if you can make massive generalisations about people who voted to leave Europe ... because people voted to leave Europe for all sorts of different reasons, and it *wasn't just racists* who voted to leave Europe ... *Cunts* did as well ... *stupid fucking cunts*. Racists and cunts.'

It is both an exaggeration of his previous vulgarity and a set up for a dialectic with a new (pedantic) voice, with nasal emphasis: "*and people* with legitimate anxieties about ever closer ties to Europe". Lee contemplates how members of his audience might write in to express these "legitimate" concerns, and he compares them to other types of voter, who may have simply wanted "bendy bananas", and not this "chaotic inferno of hate". The character of Stewart Lee clearly has disdain for Brexit voters, but the comedy sketch has also permitted different voices into the discussion. This culminates in a typically scatological sketch about an article he wrote in *The Observer*:

'I wrote, "Voting to leave Europe as a protest vote is a bit like shitting your hotel bed as a protest against bad service and then realising you now have to sleep in a shitted bed." And my friend Ian, my best friend, Leave voter, he said to me, "your metaphor doesn't make sense Stew", he said, "by your own admission, the EU is institutionally flawed, and freedom of movement can lead to exploitation of the labour market. So in a way", he said, "there's already some shit in the bed." And I said, "Yes Ian, but if there's already some shit in the bed, you don't fix that by doing even more shit, into the already shatted bed." And my friend Ian said, "No you would move into a different bed", and I said, "Yes Ian, but what if that different bed, instead of some shit, has got Boris Johnson in it?" And my friend Ian reluctantly conceded that he would remain in the original shatted bed.'

Conclusion

Comedy yields an interesting perspective on the performative politics of Brexit. Discourses of the comedy politician and the comedy establishment have emerged from and partly entrenched the divisive nature of public discussion. Ideas about 'proper' 'rational' politics have overlain stereotypes of stupid racist Leave voters, while quasi-critical discourses on the 'comedy class' have fostered a conspiratorial view of the 'liberal establishment'. However, beyond a vision of comedy as joking for our side, I have also sought to argue that there is, within comedy, a capacity for reflexivity and adaptation; that the language of politics provided by comedy can live with the 'dangers' of stereotype, the close proximity between the 'funny' and 'unfunny'.

In certain circumstances, this reflexive potential can allow for an alternative discourse that reflects our own positionality within a changing context. This might be read into the qualified dialogue envisaged in Stewart Lee's routine, where different arguments for Leave are situated, engaged, in terms of political consequences as well as *ad hominem* stereotypes. Or else, Geoff Norcott has spoken of an altogether more ambitious vision of dissensus: "This is one of the great things about Brexit, it's a re-set, it's a year zero moment for politics and a reminder that democracy means everybody's got skin in the game." For example, one of the great comedy successes of the post-Brexit period has been the rise of *The Mash Report*, a satirical news show fronted by Nish Kumar that has done much both to reflect the gendered and racialized experiences of Brexit, while retaining a polyphonic editorial line that includes pro-Brexit comedians like Norcott. Thus a radical view of the changing context might be that it is potentially far more inclusive because of, *not despite*, the divisive nature of discourse? However, I conclude this chapter by pointing to the letter that Stewart Lee (2018b) wrote to his fans as a sign of the everyday global politics at stake in comedy:

> I am not doing a new stand-up show until the Autumn of 2019, which will then tour, far less than usual, until Spring 2020 and then it's done.... I do not intend to ever do the numbers I did for the *Content Provider* tour again.... I need to do a year or so of dad stuff at home, see some music and

comedy and films and hills and rivers. & get fit. & thwart intestinal fate. & I need to have a think about where to go with stand-up with me in my 50s as *the '70s/'80s cultural consensus that shaped me dissolves* and the darkness rises.

One of the points that the discourse of the 'comedy establishment' maybe got right is that humour performs within a context, and the divisive nature of Brexit can be read as a sign that the context is changing. While some argue that 'liberal comedians' are irrevocably tied to an establishment discourse, this chapter has argued that this ignores the importance of doing 'difficult comedy' as well as the capacity of (some) comedians to reflect on their own positionality within the changing consensus. At the risk of stating the obvious, a vision of British comedy that was permanently tied to a myth of resistance to Thatcher's Britain, or Blair's moralization of global politics, is likely of poor utility for engaging the politics of a post-Brexit form of globalization.

7

The Globalization of Comic Resistance?

Introduction

This book has engaged with the practice and politics of everyday global resistance through a performative study of the emergence of British comedy. Against instrumental and critical approaches to the role of comedy and resistance in global politics, I argue that we need to pay more attention to the productive elements of humour. Too often, the study of comedy is limited by a particular vision of politics, whether state-centric and driven by a normative ontology of satirical engagement, or universalist and based on a quite demanding view of emancipation through subversion. Instead, by tracing a more performative account of comic resistance, the book suggested we should move away from questions of whether this or that joke can make an impact, or spark revolutionary change. Everyday comic resistances perform *within* a context of global social power relations. While certain jokes, in certain circumstances, may question, subvert, or otherwise undermine the everyday hierarchies of global market life, others may work to affirm such exclusions, or else provide a socially resonant, if potentially violent, mode of inclusion. Simply put, comedy does different things in different circumstances and that is precisely why it is political. By adopting this more open understanding of comedy 'as' politics, my framework of analysis has in turn licensed a more proliferative understanding of what comedy and humour can be/do. As Berlant and Ngai (2017: 235) argue:

> comedy isn't just an anxiogenic tableau of objects disrupted
> by status shifting, collapse and persistence, the disruption

by difference, or a veering between the tiny and the large. Nor is it just a field of narrative expectation punctuated by the surprise of laughter or vertiginous enjoyment. It is also epistemologically troubling, drawing insecure boundaries as though it were possible to secure confidence about object ontology or the value of an 'us' versus all its others.

British comedy seems a particularly fascinating case of an 'epistemologically troubling' discourse because so much of its focus has been upon the limits of Britishness: the ridiculous arrogance, the elitism, the racism and so on. Ironically, this critical reflexivity seems to be the very basis of its commercial success. How such an ambiguous vernacular is recuperated, re-phrased or re-imagined is a complex question of politics and the political that eludes easy resolution. The book has therefore developed a contingent understanding of British comedy that traces the emergence of this everyday vernacular of global resistance. It is in the details of humour, the various movements within comedy, what people find funny or unfunny and so on that we can locate the politics of resistance. Thus, instead of focusing on one or other comedian as a 'vanguard' of political change, my approach is more concerned with the emergence of British comedy over time; how jokes reference each other, or the way comedians contribute to a 'style' or 'form'. Rendered thus, the rich tradition of British comedy speaks to the emergence of a language of satirical resistance inflected with specific qualities and characteristics that both reflect *and embody* the everyday politics of globalization.

British comedy is global politics. Previous chapters have identified how the emergence of the 'satire boom' used comedy to reflect upon the experience of imperial decline; the way alternative comedy formed dissent against neoliberal deregulation; and how irony sought to subvert the media spectacle and the moral consensus on globalization. These comic resistances were not assessed in terms of whether they 'helped elect a left-wing government', or if they 'adequately subverted the class relations of global capitalism'. Instead, the circulation and success of these new modes of comic resistance were rendered *as a site* of global politics per se. For all that this vernacular of resistance creates opportunities for inclusion and justice, it also valorizes 'particular' modes of market life that limit our ability to think about and enact alternatives. From the white male, elite 'clubby' world of satire, to the media-savvy and market-friendly form of alternative comedy that made its peace with mainstream success by embracing market-friendly tropes of diversity and global charity, the book has therefore traced a far more ambiguous and embodied politics of globalization. Simply put, the everyday vernacular of comic resistance does not succeed or fail, emancipate or tranquillize. Rather, it provides a space, a language, a set of practices and intuitive understandings that can inform (but do not sanctify) the political agency for engagement with(in) global politics.

At one level, this has involved an intimate story about how particular comedians have contested the commodification of humour, such as Alexei Sayle, or else sought to deal with the question of ethical responsibility entailed in irony. This is therefore a contribution to the study of comedy and politics that seeks to develop an understanding of the comedian as a political actor and thinker in their own right: that is, not as someone who is only incidentally useful to political strategy. At another level, the previous chapters have discussed how the emergent vernacular of comic resistance can proliferate across genres and generations. In this sense, British comedy carries a fugitive quality, always eluding its own commodification and normalization. Sometimes this is a story of direct oppositions and contests, as per charges within comic movements that satire was posh and (post-)imperialist, or that irony was blokey and offensive. At other times, this is a simple matter of accidental re-use for alternative purposes, as per satirical memes and hashtags, or the influence of British irony on genres like graffiti (Brassett, 2009). Everyday comic resistances thus proliferate new modes of global market subjectivity, new practices of inclusion/exclusion and – importantly – new ways of being political in global context.

In essence, a broad objective of the book has been to refigure the 'large' and 'systemic' question of globalization as part of everyday lived experience; seeking to reflect the hierarchies of social difference that both emerge from and produce its logics and rationalities. In this way, as previous chapters argued, the everyday practices of British comedy are deeply informed by – and productive of – the contingent experience of globalization. Whether considering the (psychological) negotiation of imperial decline, the politicization of alternative comedy in the turn against neoliberalism, or the nuanced and open-ended resistances to the media spectacle and market subjectivity afforded by irony and radical comedy, the history of British comedy has routinely engaged with questions of what globalization is and how to think its politics. Along the way, of course, it has also actively performed many of its logics – of post-imperial angst, of commodity, of celebrity and the mediatization of global politics. In critical terms, therefore, the vernacular of British comedy has also reproduced the everyday hierarchies of social difference that pervade globalization. At stake in the move to value comic resistance is a recognition of some uncomfortable truths. Comedians are often white, male, rich (if successful); and, relatedly, jokes can still be exclusionary, violent, racist and misogynist. The contingent possibility that emerges in this analysis is ultimately 'just' a language, a vernacular of resistance through which satirical subjects 'might' perform differently.

This final chapter will therefore seek to consolidate and extend the analysis by asking a forward-looking set of questions about the globalization of comic resistance and the chances for *a further politicization* of the vernacular. Discussion is divided into two sections that outline the potential research agendas that might emerge from this project. The first section will address the globalization of British comedy in terms of the proliferation of comedians and producers, films and series that have succeeded on the global market. While there is a tendency to portray the globalization of British comedy as an archetypal illustration of the limits of materialism, not least among British comedians who 'don't make it', I will suggest some reasons to complicate this picture. The second section will address a more critical set of questions about whether the vernacular of British comedy can be *globalized* in a second sense, one that de-centres the role of heroic white men in the progressive myth of British comedy. In short, can the vernacular of British comedy provide the resources and tools required to facilitate the agency to resist its own hegemonic and imperial qualities, centred as it (still) is on overlapping intersections of nationality, class, race and gender?

1 The British are coming (again)

For many of the comedy acts considered in this book the idea of a 'globalization' of British comedy is commonly understood in terms of commercial success 'in America'. Indeed, the early excitement that surrounded the satire boom was partly based on the reflected glory that *Beyond the Fringe* and *Monty Python* had 'made it' on the other side of the Atlantic. Typically, of course, this valorization of comedians 'if' – and sometimes 'because' – they are popular in the US does not hold sway with all sections of the industry. The Pythons probably experienced the high point of American success, becoming stars on the big screen, playing the Hollywood Bowl, and remaining influential among the writers of modern satires like *South Park*. However, the popularity of subsequent comedians has often been a focus of chagrin. On the one hand, there is the eternal return of the instrumental critique that cites the model of Dudley Moore's long list of mediocre rom-coms to lament how good comedians go to America to 'cash in'. On the other hand, there is an element of jealousy or snobbery in certain critiques. The long held, yet largely forgotten idea that Americans don't 'get' irony can sometimes underpin a sense that the US market is where you go if you can't hack the 'serious' world of British comedy. Much like punk bands that get 'big in Japan', comedians like James Corden and Ricky Gervais are sometimes sneered at for their US careers. In a word, the relationship between British comedy and the dilemma of success in America can (again) reveal quite a bit about the post-imperial angst that infuses so much of the tradition.

Beyond such cultural difficulties, however, the globalization of British comedy through US media platforms is a crucial issue for thinking about the politics of comic resistance. At the risk of stating the obvious, the translation of British comedy onto global markets is not just about commercial success. Money is important, of course. As Armando Iannucci (2012) remarked, US media corporations are important players in the globalization of British comedy because they have just got "lots and lots" of money, but this also has implications for *the way* they work: they can buy time to develop a concept, entertain radically different levels of output, and underwrite a large roster of actors and writers. As a model of comedy production, this can create interesting alternatives. While more writers, more episodes and bigger stars, usually translates into higher viewing figures, there is also an opportunity to foster and support innovation. This contrasts with a UK system of support, which relies on a logic of sink or swim, where there is very little opportunity to support new acts, and hence a predilection amongst broadcasters for established names and bankable formats such as sitcoms and panel shows. Key examples of the benefits of this alternative production model are the US version of *The Office*, which syndicated a famously short and limited satire in the UK to produce a multi-episode, multi-season format, that flourished across platforms and countries; as well as the long rise of John Oliver, who had worked for several years on the UK circuit, but was later developed through appearances on *The Daily Show* to a point where he could anchor his own *Last Week Tonight with John Oliver*. To underline, these are not just important stories of instrumental success for British comedy but speak to the possibility of a fundamental re-imagination, allowing for the long-term development of strong female comics like Mindy Kaling in *The Office*, and, arguably, one of the most significant re-statements of the power of news satire since the 'satire boom' by John Oliver. Oliver's long-form satires have allowed him to develop densely researched, fact-heavy, monologues that bridge irony and investigative journalism to perform a veritable public education service on subjects like the role of private companies in prisons, transgender politics and, of course, Trump.

More critically, then, the globalization of comic resistance has allowed British comedy to look beyond itself, perhaps 'improving' it in certain ways. For instance, despite notable exceptions, the highly nuanced and layered nature of many acts within British comedy can sometimes mean the audience is required do *quite a bit of work*. On the one hand, this can be one of the more enjoyable and satisfying aspects of British comedy, for example, when we watch a Stewart Lee routine and enter into an imaginative play of whether we are 'the good, clever' ones in the audience, and if we remember Thatcher's role in a *Scooby Doo* film about cuts to the welfare state. On the other hand, British comedy can sometimes come across as slightly 'difficult', where the parochial nature of comic resistances to global logics and rationalities is actually quite niche. While this is precisely the critical point – that globalization works via the routinization of logics and practices of the ordinary and the mundane, that is, through advertising, morality and media spectacle, it is important to recognize that cultural awareness of the British experience of globalization may not always translate. At the very least, only certain audiences will understand the cultural significance of Alexei Sayle's diatribes against Evian, or Iannucci's references to Curly Wurlys and Seb Coe.

The globalization of British comedy can therefore contribute to the expansion of the scope of ethical concern and indeed the communication of comic resistances to globalization. Two very particular examples can illustrate the importance and difficulty of practising comic resistances on a global scale. First, the satirical work of Sacha Baron Cohen has arguably had the most significant cut-through to global audiences through his ability to create a sense of spectacle. While Ali G received some attention in the US, it was Baron Cohen's translation of another character, Borat, to a film-length narrative that drove his global rise, garnering massive international audiences and even diplomatic attention. Borat is notionally a Kazakh documentary film-maker who intends to learn about the American dream. While the postmodern clown technique remains, there is a sense in which, as Rob Saunders (2009) argues, Borat moves into a realm of minstrelsy or basic race comedy. Borat introduces himself and his country in terms that play on the 'backwardness' of its people. We meet the town rapist ("naughty, naughty"), his sister, who he kisses passionately, announcing that she is the "No. 4 prostitute in all of Kazakhstan". Then his journey across America provides a narrative structure that allows him to string together a series of interactive satires, where he essentially plays on the way different Americans 'take' his character: if they find him offensive, if they reveal their own prejudices, or in some cases, if they find a way to be nice to him, while retaining a belief in basic values of equality and liberty.

While there is an interesting construction at work in Sacha Baron Cohen's humour, indeed, one which speaks to the potential of ironic resistance examined in Chapter 4, it is also clear that the move to a global stage intensifies the politics of reception. The essentially ambiguous nature of irony over political correctness means the humour can be relayed in reactionary terms; that people might recycle his jokes about 'the jew', how a feminist doesn't smile, or describing a black politician as 'a genuine chocolate face' (for example in *Borat*, 2006). On this view, there is a genuine question as to whether the successful generalization of irony over political correctness is desirable at all, or if Baron Cohen has taken an initially clever joke and simply packaged it for 'frat boys'? However, by commodifying irony in this way, Baron Cohen has also popularized the performative stunt on a global stage. A form of interactive satire that Chris Morris experimented with, using low-level politicians and c-list celebrities on *Brass Eye*, has arguably been taken forward and developed substantially. In subsequent shows like *Who Is America?* Baron Cohen was able to dupe no less a figure than Dick Cheney, who he convinced to sign some waterboarding equipment as a memento. In another, further iteration of the satire of global charity, Baron Cohen persuaded a US reality-TV star to promote an Ebola charity 'virtually', that is, to have photos taken in a hazmat suit on green screen, which could then be superimposed on images of humanitarian actions ("It was good because I saved 6,000 people").

Second, then, building from this possibility, one broad way in which British comedy has globalized most effectively is in the turn to interactive satire on a global stage, especially via commodity and celebrity subversion. Examples of this abound in the history of British comedy of course. While Chris Morris pioneered the use of the form to supplement larger narrative deconstructions of the mediatized spectacle, other comedians have been more direct. Notable here is the work of Mark Thomas, who perfected the art of situating himself within corporate events in order to ask difficult or awkward questions about arms sales or the privatization of the health system. More recently, Simon Brodkin, aka Lee Nelson, has developed a kind of interactive satirical event on the global stage, famously approaching the head of FIFA (Fédération Internationale de Football Association) Sepp Blatter and throwing money into the air above his head. To underline, while Chris Morris's work required a significant amount of thought and 'argument' to draw out the satirical point, Brodkin's work is *injected directly* into the global media form itself. In another example, he infiltrated Turnberry golf course and managed to get close enough to a Trump press conference to give him '65 Swastika golf balls' that he rolled on the ground at his feet.

It might be suggested that such interactive satires run the risk of generating the same ambiguities as Sacha Baron Cohen, an easy 'gotcha' moment for those who get the joke, which licenses a more cynical and confrontational attitude towards politicians. Indeed, at least one critique of *Who Is America?* is that some of the set-ups became intensely cruel and difficult to watch. However, in other moments there can be a productive politics to how the jokes circulate, get discussed and challenge preconceptions. For example, one issue that Brodkin has highlighted in interviews is his treatment by the police. We are often trained to think about the police as basic instrument of power, indeed, Brodkin has spoken of his experiences of being arrested and locked up after such events. On different occasions, though, they have treated him differently. After the Trump-swastika-golf-balls incident, they made it clear to him that he was lucky he hadn't been shot by US security. After another stunt, where he dressed up as a young Tory at the Conservative Party conference and presented Theresa May with a P-45 during her speech, he feared the worst. Arrested and removed for questioning by a very senior police officer, she asked how he got so close to the Prime Minister. When he explained that he had simply applied via the Conservative Party website using his own name, they lost interest and passed him down to standard police who drove him to the station, where they discharged him with the line: 'That was very funny what you did', then gave him a lift home and got a selfie (Brodkin, 2017).

Perhaps, the most high-profile example of this form of 'big appeal' interactive satire is provided by Ricky Gervais. While Gervais has lost some of his aura with UK audiences, for whom the mock humble/arrogant schtick struggles to survive his massive success, he has nevertheless retained a believable lower status amongst the audience and winners of the Golden Globes, which he regularly presents. While the format is in the US tradition of a public 'roast', Gervais brings his own certain particular dynamic to the performance, so it appears as if he is interacting satirically with the media form around him. Prefacing the 2020 speech with the suggestion that it is his last year presenting, so he "doesn't care", he bookends: "let's go out with a bang, let's have a laugh, at your expense... Remember, they're just jokes, we're all gonna die soon, and there's no sequel."[1] He opens with some paedophile material about "Two Popes", moving into race: "Many talented people of colour were snubbed in major categories, unfortunately there's nothing we can do about that, the Hollywood foreign press are all very, very racist. So … 5th time [he gestures at himself]."

The layers of irony are typically hard to decipher, not least because the standard critique that Gervais is racist, has been woven within the routine. As Chapters 4 and 5 argued, the liminal form that emerges is unlikely to provide an easy resolution of the dilemmas of global market life that it performs and recycles for laughs. However, I would suggest that an important moment of instability in the commodity form is articulated in Gervais' repeated demonstration of the way corporate media often tries to insulate itself with tropes of diversity. For example:

> 'Apple roared into the TV game with the Morning show … a superb drama about the importance of dignity and doing the right thing, made by a company that runs sweatshops in China. So … [addressing the audience directly] well you say you're woke but the companies you work for, unbelievable, Apple, Amazon, Disney. If Isis started a streaming service, you'd call your agent, wouldn't you?'[2]

In Gervais' speech, the point is made to qualify actors who might seek to 'virtue signal' when they get their awards, but I would suggest that the demonstration of wider political economic connections between the media and structures of global production is also a significant moment of comic resistance, made on a global stage through the celebrity spectacle.

2 The state of British comedy

As British comedy ebbs and flows on the global stage, it is also important to reflect on its status as a national vernacular of everyday resistance. While many of the positive elements in British comedy relate to the mobilization of the small and the mundane to tell a critical story about the hierarchies of social difference that persist through globalization, there is also a sense in which this resistant vernacular has recuperated one of the most problematic elements of globalization: its

---

[1]   Ricky Gervais at the Golden Globes 2020, 9 January 2020, https://www.youtube.com/watch?v=sR6UeVptzRg (accessed 13 August 2020).

[2]   Ibid.

state form. For all that the contingencies of British imperial decline, neoliberalization, austerity and Brexit have created a vibrant and sometimes 'charged' comic vernacular, there is little doubt that it has also produced *a national* discourse. Many of the comedy acts considered in the book are cherished within the culture, viewed as 'national treasures' and even, curiously, members of the actual establishment with OBEs, MBEs and knighthoods. Indeed, as previous chapters have argued, despite manifest and ongoing commitments to values of equality and diversity, many of the prevailing voices in British comedy continue to be white, male, English.

To some extent, this state of affairs was somewhat envisaged in the theoretical framework of resistance that I outlined in Chapter 1. Everyday practices of resistance work within power, often drawing upon and refiguring power relations, rather than overcoming or otherwise sanctifying them. Equally, the turn to the everyday is not a simple case of prioritizing non-elite agency for resistance, but rather involves a set of political questions about how the 'everyday' is formed through ongoing global power relations. As such, I have tried to trace a more ambiguous story of how the resistant vernacular of British comedy is somehow both recalcitrant and valorized. On this view, the progressive myth of British comedy is also a story about how the British are *redeemable*, through irony over our failure, anger at our inequalities and so on. In this sense, the critical and resistant potentials of British comedy must also be read in line with a circumscribed vision about what it means to be British, one that is both patriarchal and raced.

Within the comedy industry, for instance, diversity is commonly promoted as a process of including a 'female comedian' or a 'black comedian'. In practical terms, this can often mean 'the' female comedian or 'the' black comedian. Ironically, as Chapter 3 argued, this is partly a product of how alternative comedy was mainstreamed in the 1980s, weaving its belief that comedy should 'not be racist' and 'not be sexist' into the dominant market logic. To channel Alexei Sayle one last time, it speaks of a peculiar faith in capitalism to regulate the commodity form of comedy as if such regulation can eliminate all contentious social and political subjects. While this can lead to well-meaning discussions in the public sphere about diversity on panel shows like *Mock the Week*, the fact of having this conversation can perform an air of legitimacy that distracts from the substance *and experience* of comedy in terms of race and gender. For example, the inclusion of one or two women on a panel show does little to problematize the masculinist discourse of 'literal' points scoring. More critically, it fails to reflect the experience of becoming the market subject of a 'female comedian' or a 'black comedian' in the first place. In a recent interview with *The Voice*, Lenny Henry spoke about his childhood experience of jokes:

> 'I think that what happens with migrants is this sense of assimilation that you have to do when you move from one country to another country, and we all migrants do it, you arrive somewhere and you go, "ok yeh, well I speak my home language but I've very quickly got to learn how to speak here otherwise I'm gonna get stomped on." You know forces, bureaucracy, and people, they're gonna take liberties with me unless I figure out how to communicate. So you learn to communicate. Then you think "oh ok, I need to learn to communicate better than that because they're taking the piss out of the way I talk", so after a while you learn to speak better. Then you have to figure out humour. Oh to communicate really well I got to figure out what [...] jokes people are running, cos if I don't figure out what the joke is, *I'm gonna be* the joke. So then you learn to assimilate even more and by the time you've been here for a year or two years or three years, you know the banter and you know the jokes you know how people talk, you know what they eat, you can hang out and … you've got that sense of belonging.'[3]

Henry's recollections speak of the experience of becoming British *through humour*, through jokes, through banter. While I would not like to generalize his experience as model, and indeed in the interview he does not portray this history as a particularly exclusionary experience, it is important to reflect on the global social relations that are 'entrenched' through comedic identity. For every black, Asian, female or disabled comic that gets in through the door of diversity and inclusion, there are countless experiences of exclusionary humour, or/and the idea that you have to be good at humour to be included.

How do we resist these hierarchies of comic resistance? At one level, there are pathologies in the industry. Previous chapters discussed the common and ongoing practice of men playing female parts, jokes about women, the sexual stereotyping of female experience and so on. Equally, the older tradition of white comedians playing black parts through 'black face' and exaggerated voices has never really gone away. Recently, in

---

3   Lenny Henry, interview with *The Voice*, 19 November 2019, https://www.youtube.com/watch?v=9wgD-lj5v9A (accessed 13 August 2020).

response to the comedian Lee Francis apologizing for his use of black face in Bo Selecta, a social media discussion on the racial limits of British comedy led to the removal of *Little Britain* from Netflix.[4] On this view, the importance and politics of exercising ethical responsibility in relation to irony can also be engaged by global publics, not just comedians and writers. Whether and how we might politicize, rather than merely regulate the industry is a question that calls for alternative conceptions of agency for change; either within the comedy industry itself, or beyond through activist groups and in the arts sector, more broadly. In productive terms, the inclusive production models of the BBC and Channel 4 should continue to recognize and support comedians like Dane Baptiste, Guz Khan, Doc Brown, as well as shows like *Man Like Mobeen*, *Chewing Gum*, and promising experiments with rising stars like *The Mash Report* and *The Lateish Show with Mo Gilligan*.

At another level, though, I would also point to the emergence of alternative comic pathways. Too often, the notion of success or failure within British comedy is understood in terms of the big commission, the TV gig or the Netflix special. Not only does this subject artists to the problematic logics of being the '(insert minority)' comedian, for instance, as Stephen K Amos remarked: 'It's one in one out.'[5] But it also ignores the creative potential of alternative models of production afforded by new technologies and social media. Although Chapters 5 and 6 tried to take some account of the proliferation of social media memes and hashtags, this was figured in terms of a democratization of the global public sphere. While important, the emerging overlaps between new technologies, social media and comedy also perform new modes of satirical production that hold important implications and possibilities for resisting the centralizing tendencies of the comedy industry. Indeed, to take one example from above, the emergence of *The Mash Report* initially built on the experience of internet satire account *The Daily Mash*, and, once established on BBC, it then continued to cultivate audiences through the circulation of clips, which often reached an audience far in excess of the original TV show (Kumar, 2018). More critically, I would argue, this productive milieu also holds out a potential

---

[4]   'Little Britain Pulled from I-Player and Netflix because "Times Have Changed"', 9 June 2020, https://www.bbc.co.uk/news/entertainment-arts-52983319 (accessed 17 June 2020).

[5]   'From Real McCoy to Famalam: How the Black British Sketch Show Came of Age', 9 April 2018, https://www.theguardian.com/tv-and-radio/2018/apr/09/famalam-akemnji-ndifornyen-tom-marshall-black-sketch-shows-tv-comedy (accessed 10 August 2020).

for resisting the everyday hierarchies of social difference that pervade the market form of comedy by actively disrupting both the structure of production and the relationship between performer and audience.

Drawing these points together, the fugitive qualities of humour, the proliferative potential across genres and subjects, can also underwrite the emergence of alternative economic models. Feminist satire has been pronounced in this new milieu with a range of podcasts, online magazines, and popular hashtags emerging around the themes of gender politics; inter alia the *Guilty Feminist*, *ManWhoHasItAll*, *Dear Joan and Jericha*. Indeed, there is also an overlap with feminist academics through agendas like 'Congratulations You Have An All Male Panel' and 'Women Also Know Stuff'. Online satire is bound up with a productive conception of the audience, one which actively relies upon user engagement, retweets, likes, controversy and newspaper articles. For example, *ManWhoHasItAll* is structured around a basic but incredibly effective subversion: what if you take all the cultural anxieties imputed onto modern women and cast them through a man? The result is an immediate and easily adapted perspective on the instability and ridiculousness of liberal gender norms. To take at random some tweets:

- My friend is a history teacher. She's compiling a list of great historical figures and she needs to add a male to the list. Suggestions?
- TODAY'S DEBATE: Why can't we believe unmarried childless men are happy?
- TODAY'S QUESTION: What do boys look for in a cycle helmet?
- 'Reading a wonderful little collection of men's poetry taught me how to respect men' Claire, CEO. Thanks for being such a wonderful ally Claire, we need more good women like you.
- I'm pitching an article to the Men's section of a tabloid about the problem with men's voices and what they can do about it. Suggestions?

Indeed, this last tweet had a funny reply from another user: 'Why are men talking? If it's in the workplace they should do the following: 1) Don't talk unless asked a direct question 2) Speak in a low pleasant modulated tone 3) Smile, as he has been acknowledged, and thank the person asking the question.' This capacity for different forms of engagement in and through feminist satire is perhaps a more challenging issue for thinking about comic resistance. Increasingly the audience is a productive element in satire: feminist satire is a space of conversation and engagement where the joke is essentially uncontrollable and subject to circulation, adaptation and new iterations. For example, there are early signs that the turn to long-form, spoken-word, podcast formats can be a space for developing these 'alternative economies of alternative comedy'. On the one hand, there is a pronounced ethos of reciprocity, whereby comedians can both build their respective fan bases and foster new talent in a supportive environment. On the other hand, the audience involvement is more intimate and involved, where podcasts can be funded in a number of ways, by people paying for tickets on 'the night', or through crowd funding through new infrastructures like Patreon. The point is that the public sphere of comedy can be de-centred from the national media, indeed, from the generalist comedy club that can carry the kinds of exclusionary identity norms that discipline comic resistance in particular ways.

Conclusion

In conclusion, this closing chapter of the book has tried to draw some different threads together by focusing on the future challenges to the everyday vernacular of comic resistance. Against a vision of globalizing British comedy as an inevitable 'selling out' of the form, I have tried to complicate the picture through a discussion of the importance of alternative production models and the power of commodity subversion through the medium of the performative stunt. In terms of the myth of British comedy as progressive, I have tried to qualify and decentre the state-centric limits of the vernacular. While my approach has foregrounded the complex and ambiguous entwinement between everyday practices of comic resistance and the hierarchies of social difference that pervade globalization, this chapter has also sought to imagine ways to think beyond such limits. In particular, the everyday racial and gendered hierarchies of exclusion, as well as the terms of inclusion, were an ongoing set of questions for the politics of comic resistance. Promising lines of regulation, alternative visions of production and the growing role of technologies and audiences in the substance of comedy were discussed in terms of both mitigating current pathologies and imagining other ways of practising comic resistance.

Bibliography

Aitken, R. (2007) *Performing Capital: Toward a Cultural Economy of Popular and Global Finance*. Basingstoke: Palgrave Macmillan.

Amoore, L. and Hall, A. (2013) 'The clown at the gates of the camp: sovereignty, resistance and the figure of the fool', *Security Dialogue* 44: 93–110.

Andrews, M. (1998) 'Butterflies and caustic asides', in S. Wagg (ed.) *Because I tell a Joke or Two: Comedy, Politics and Social Difference*. London: Routledge.

Anonymous (2016) 'Alt-right: online poison nearly turned me into a racist', *The Guardian*, 28 November 2016, https://www.theguardian.com/commentisfree/2016/nov/28/alt-right-online-poison-racist-bigot-sam-harris-milo-yiannopoulos-islamophobia (accessed 24 August 2020).

Bakhtin, M. (1984) *Rabelais and His World*. Bloomington, IN: Indiana University Press.

Bakker, I. (2007) 'Social reproduction and the constitution of a gendered political economy', *New Political Economy*, 12(4): 541–56.

Bedford, K. (2019) *Bingo Capitalism: The Law and Political Economy of Everyday Gambling*, Oxford: Oxford University Press.

Bergson, H. (1911) *Laughter: An Essay on the Meaning of the Comic*. Copenhagen and Los Angeles: Green Integer.

Berlant, L. and Ngai, S. (2017) 'Comedy has issues', *Critical Inquiry* 43: 233–49.

Best, J. and Paterson, M. (eds) (2010) *Cultural Political Economy*. New York: Routledge.

Billig, M. (2005) *Laughter and Ridicule: Towards a Social Critique of Humour*. London: Sage.

Bleiker, R. (2000) *Popular Dissent, Human Agency and Global Politics*. Cambridge: Cambridge University Press.

Brassett, J. (2009) 'British irony, global justice: a pragmatic reading of Chris Brown, Banksy, and Ricky Gervais', *Review of International Studies* 35(1): 219–45.

Brassett, J. (2016) 'British comedy, global resistance: Russell Brand, Charlie Brooker, and Stewart Lee', *European Journal of International Relations* 22(1): 168–91.

Brassett, J. (2018) *Affective Politics of the Global Event: Trauma and the Resilient Market Subject*. Abingdon: Routledge.

Brassett, J. (2018a) 'British comedy and the politics of resistance', in J. Webber (ed.) *The Joke is On Us: Political Comedy in Late Neoliberal Times*. New York: Lexington Books, pp 177–92.

Brassett, J. and Heine, F. (forthcoming) 'Men behaving badly: representations of masculinity in post-global financial crisis cinema', *International Feminist Journal of Politics*.

Brassett, J. and Rethel, R. (2015) 'Sexy money: the hetero-normative politics of global finance', *Review of International Studies*, 41(3): 429–49.

Brassett, J. and Smith, W. (2010) 'Deliberation and global civil society: agency, arena, affect', *Review of International Studies* 36(2): 413–30.

Brassett, J. and Sutton, A. (2017) 'British satire, everyday politics: Chris Morris, Armando Iannucci, and Charlie Brooker', *British Journal of Politics and International Relations* 19(2): 245–62.

Brassett, J. Browning, C. and O'Dwyer, M. (forthcoming) 'EU've Got to be Kidding: Anxiety, Humour and Ontological Security', *Global Society*.

British Comedy Guide (2016) 'Alexei Sayle Talks to Stewart Lee', 3 March 2016, https://www.youtube.com/watch?v=lLsJu7rqs8o (accessed 4 September 2019).

Brodkin, S. (2017) 'Interview with Richard Herring', *Richard Herring's Leicester Square Theatre Podcast*.

Brooker, C. (2014) '*Benefits Street*: poverty porn or just the latest target for pent-up British fury?' *The Guardian*, 12 January 2004, https://www.theguardian.com/commentisfree/2014/jan/12/benefits-street-poverty-porn-british-fury (accessed 24 August 2020).

Butler, J. (1993) *Bodies That Matter: On the Discursive Limitations of 'Sex'*. London: Routledge.

Butler, J. (1999) *Gender Trouble: Feminism and the Subversion of Identity*. London: Routledge.

Butler, J. (2005) *Giving an Account of Oneself*. New York: Fordham University Press.

Butler, J. (2010) 'Performative agency', *Journal of Cultural Economy* 3(2): 147–61.

Carpenter, H. (2000) *That Was the Satire that Was: The Satire Boom of the 1960s*, London: Victor Gollanncz.

Cerny, P. (1997) 'Paradoxes of the competition state: the dynamics of political globalization', *Government and Opposition* 32(2): 251–71.

Chandra, U. (2015) 'Introduction: Rethinking subaltern resistance', *Journal of Contemporary Asia* 45(4): 563–73.

Coe, J. (2013) 'Sinking giggling into the sea', *London Review of Books* 35(14): 30–1.

Coogan, S. (2011) 'Steve Coogan: I'm a huge fan of Top Gear, but this time I've had enough', *The Guardian*, 5 February 2011, https://www.theguardian.com/tv-and-radio/2011/feb/05/top-gear-offensive-steve-coogan (accessed 24 August 2020).

Cook, W. (2001) *The Comedy Store: The club that Changed British Comedy.* London: Little, Brown and Co.

Corbyn, J. (2015) Speech to the Labour Party Annual Conference, http://press.labour.org.uk/post/130135691169/speech-by-jeremy-corbyn-to-labour-partyannual (accessed 10 May 2016).

Critchley, S (1999) 'Comedy and finitude: displacing the tragic-heroic paradigm in philosophy and psychoanalysis', *Constellations*, 6(1): 108–22.

Critchley, S. (2002) *On Humour.* London: Routledge.

Davies, M. (2016) 'Everyday life as critique: revisiting the everyday in IPE with Henri Lefebvre and postcolonialism', *International Political Sociology* 10(1): 22–38.

Davies, W. (2016) 'Thoughts on the sociology of Brexit', Goldsmiths, Political Economy Research Centre, http://www.perc.org.uk/project_posts/thoughts-on-the-sociology-of-brexit/

Dean, J. (2019) 'Sorted for memes and gifs: visual media and everyday digital politics', *Political Studies Review* 17(3): 255–66.

De Goede, M. (2005) 'Carnival of money: politics of dissent in an era of globalising finance,' in L. Amoore (ed.) *Global Resistance Reader,* London: Routledge.

Denby, D. (2010) *Snark.* New York: Simon and Schuster.

Dodds, K. and Kirby, P. (2013) 'It's not a laughing matter: critical geopolitics, humour and unlaughter', *Geopolitics* 18(1): 45–59.

Dryzek, J. (2006) *Deliberative Global Politics: Discourse and Democracy in a Divided World.* Cambridge: Polity.

Elias, J. and Rai, S. (2018) 'Feminist everyday political economy: space, time, and violence', *Review of International Studies* 45(2): 1–20.

Elias, J. and Roberts, A. (2010) 'Feminist global political economies of the everyday: from bananas to bingo', *Globalizations* 13(6): 787–800.

Enloe, C. (2014) *Bananas, Beaches and Bases: Making Feminist Sense of International Politics.* Berkeley: University of California Press.

Evening Standard (2015) 'King of Satire: Armando Iannucci on Veep, Jeremy Corbyn and his new film about the last days of Stalin', 8 October 2015, http://www.standard.co.uk/lifestyle/london-life/king-of-satire-armando-iannucci-on-veepjeremy-corbyn-and-his-new-film-about-the-last-days-of-stalin-a3085421.html

Fielding, S. (2011) 'Comedy and politics: the great debate', 29 September, http://blogs.nottingham.ac.uk/politics/2011/09/29/comedy-and-politics-the-great-debate (accessed 12 August 2020).

Fielding, S. (2014a) *A State of Play: British Politics on Screen, Stage and Page, from Anthony Trollope to The Thick of It*. London: Bloomsbury.

Fielding, S. (2014b) 'New Labour, "sleaze" and television drama', *British Journal of Politics and International Relations* 16(2): 326–48.

Flinders, M. (2013) 'Dear Russell Brand', OUP blog, 30 October, http://blog.oup.com/2013/10/dear-russell-brand-politics-comedy-jeremy-paxman/ (accessed 12 August 2020).

Foucault, M. (1990) *The History of Sexuality*, vol. 3: *The Care of the Self*. Harmondsworth: Penguin.

Foucault, M. (2007) 'What is critique?', in M. Foucault, *The Politics of Truth*, S. Lotringer (ed.), trans. L. Hochroth and C. Porter, Los Angeles, CA: Semiotext, pp 41–81.

Fox, K. (2014) *Watching the English: The Hidden Rules of English Behaviour*. London: Hodder and Stoughton.

Freud, S. (2003) *The Joke and Its Relation to the Unconscious*. London: Penguin.

Friedman, S. (2011) 'The cultural currency of a good sense of humour: British comedy and new forms of distinction', *British Journal of Sociology* 62(2): 347–70.

Gamble, A. (1994) *Britain in Decline: Economic Policy, Political Strategy and the British State*, 4th edn. London: Palgrave.

Giappone, K.B.R. (2017) 'Laughing Otherwise: comic-critical approaches in alternative comedy', *Journal for Cultural Research* 21(4): 394–413.

Grayson, K. (2018) 'Popular geopolitics and popular culture in world politics', in R. Saunders and V. Struvok (eds) *Popular Geopolitics: Plotting an Evolving Inter-discipline*. London: Routledge, pp 43–62.

Grayson, K., Davies M. and Philpott, S. (2009) 'Pop goes IR? Researching the popular culture–world politics continuum', *Politics* 29(3): 172–85.

Griffin, P. (2013) 'Gendering global finance crisis, masculinity, and responsibility', *Men and Masculinities* 16(1): 9–34.

Guillaume, X. (2011) 'Resistance and the international: the challenge of the everyday', *International Political Sociology* 5(4): 459–62.

Guillaume, X. and Huysmans, J. (2019) 'The concept of 'the everyday': ephemeral politics and the abundance of life', *International Political Sociology* 54(2): 278–96.

Halberstam, J. (2011) *The Queer Art of Failure*. Durham, NC: Duke University Press.

Hanks, R. (2000) 'The distorted world of Chris Morris', *The Independent*, http://www.independent.co.uk/news/people/profiles/the-distorted-world-of-chris-morris-281039.html (accessed 12 August 2020).

Hardy, J. (2017) 'Interview with Stuart Goldsmith', *The Comedians Comedian Podcast*, 15 May 2017.

Heath-Kelly, C. and Jarvis, L. (2017) 'Affecting terrorism: laughter, lamentation, and detestation as drives to terrorist knowledge', *International Political Sociology* 11(3): 239–56.

Herod, A. (2007) 'The agency of labour in global change: reimagining the spaces and scales of trade union praxis within a global economy', in J. Hobson and L. Seabrooke (eds) *Everyday Politics of the World Economy*. Cambridge: Cambridge University Press, pp 27–44.

Higgie, R. (2017) 'Public engagement, propaganda or both? Attitudes towards politicians on political satire and comedy programs', *International Journal of Communication* 11: 930–48.

Hobson, J. and Seabrooke, L. (eds) (2007) *Everyday Politics of the World Economy*. Cambridge: Cambridge University Press.

Holland, J. (2019) *Fictional Television and American Politics, from 9/11 to Donald Trump*. Manchester: Manchester University Press.

Horkheimer, M. and Adorno, T. (1979) *Dialectic of Enlightenment*. London: Verso.

Hunt, L. (2010) 'Near the knuckle? It nearly took my arm off! British comedy and the "new offensiveness"', *Comedy Studies* 1(2): 181–90.

Iannucci, A. (2012) 'Interview with Richard Herring', *Richard Herring's Leicester Square Theatre Podcast*, 26 June.

Iannucci, A. (2015) 'It's time for a very British revolution', *New Statesmen*, 20 April, http://www.newstatesman.com/politics/2015/04/armando-iannucci-it-s-time-very-british-revolution (accessed 12 August 2020).

Iannucci, A. (2016) 'From Trump to Boris, I wouldn't write *The Thick of It* now – politics already feels fictional enough', *New Statesman*, 11 June, http://www.newstatesman.com/politics/uk/2016/06/trump-boris-i-wouldn-t-write-thick-it-now-politics-already-feels-fictional (accessed 12 August 2020).

Innes, A. and Topinka, R. (2017) 'The politics of a poncy pillowcase': migration and borders in Coronation Street', *Politics* 37(3): 273–87.

Jameson, F. (1991) *Postmodernism, Or, The Cultural Logic of Late Capitalism.* Durham, NC: Duke University Press.

Kapoor, I. (2012) *Celebrity Humanitarianism: The Ideology of Global Charity.* London: Routledge.

Kovesi, S. (2012) 'Interview with Stewart Lee', Department of English and Modern Languages, Oxford Brookes University, 7 May, https://www.youtube.com/watch?v=8-2rVyizLt8 (accessed 19 September 2019).

Kuipers, G. (2011) 'The politics of humour in the public sphere: cartoons, power and modernity in the first transnational humour scandal', *European Journal of Cultural Studies* 14(1): 63–80.

Kumar, N. (2018) 'Interview with Richard Herring', *Richard Herring's Leicester Square Theatre Podcast.*

Langley, P. (2007) 'The uncertain subjects of Anglo-American financialization', *Cultural Critique* 65 (Winter): 66–91.

Langley, P. (2008) *The Everyday Life of Global Finance: Saving and Borrowing in Anglo America.* Oxford: Oxford University Press.

Langley, P. and Leyshon, A. (2012) 'Financial subjects: culture and materiality', *Journal of Cultural Economy* 5: 369–73.

Lee, S. (2009) *Stewart Lee's Comedy Vehicle,* Series 1 Episode 3, 'Political Correctness', 20 March 2009.

Lee, S. (2010) *How I Escaped My Certain Fate: The Life and Deaths of a Stand-up Comedian.* London: Faber and Faber.

Lee, S. (2012) 'Interview with Richard Herring', *Richard Herring's Leicester Square Theatre Podcast.*

Lee, S. (2014) *Stewart Lee's Comedy Vehicle,* Series 3, Episode 3, 'Satire', 15 March 2014.

Lee, S. (2014a) 'What to do if millions of Romanian vampires pitch camp at Marble Arch', *The Guardian,* 5 January, http://www.theguardian.com/commentisfree/2014/jan/05/romania-immigration-uk-stewart-lee?CMP=fb_gu (accessed 12 August 2020).

Lee, S. (2014b) 'Public art cant be used for adverts. But my subconscious is up for sale', *The Guardian,* 11 May 2014, https://www.theguardian.com/commentisfree/2014/may/11/public-art-adverts-subconscious-for-sale-stewart-lee (accessed: 24 August 2020).

Lee, S. (2018a) 'Content Provider', recorded live at the Palace Theatre, Southend on Sea, April, released via BBC i-Player and YouTube.

Lee S. (2018b) From the Desk of Stewart Lee: From the Metro-Lib-Elite Desk of Stew Art Lee, 2018, Message from My Brain, April 12 2018, https://www.stewartlee.co.uk/2018/04/from-the-metro-lib-elite-desk-of-stew-art-lee-may-2018/ (accessed 24 August 2020).

Lockyer, S. (ed.) (2010) *Reading Little Britain: Comedy Matters on Contemporary Television*. London: I.B Tauris.

Lockyer, S. and Attwood, F. (2009) ' "The sickest television show ever:" *Paedogeddon* and the British press', *Popular Communication* 7(1): 49–60.

Lockyer, S. and Pickering, M. (2008) 'You must be joking: the sociological critique of humour and comic media', *Sociology Compass* 2(3): 808–20.

Lockyer, S. and Pickering, M. (eds) (2009) *Beyond a Joke: The Limits of Humour*. Basingstoke: Palgrave Macmillan.

Malik, S. (2010) 'How *Little Britain* does 'race", in S. Lockyer (ed.) *Reading Little Britain: Comedy Matters on Contemporary Television*, London: IB Tauris, pp 75–94.

McCrum, R. (2000) 'Have we taken irony too far?', *The Guardian*, 10 July, https://www.theguardian.com/theguardian/2000/jul/10/features11.g21 (accessed 12 September 2019).

Meikle, G. (2012) ' "Find out exactly what to think next!": Chris Morris, *Brass Eye*, and journalistic authority', *Popular Communication* 10(1–2): 14–26.

Morreall, J. (ed.) (1987) (ed.) *The Philosophy of Laughter and Humour*. Albany, NY: SUNY Press.

Morton, A.D. (2007) 'Peasants as subaltern agents in Latin America: neoliberalism, resistance and the power of the powerless', in J. Hobson and L. Seabrooke (eds) *Everyday Politics of the World Economy*. Cambridge: Cambridge University Press, pp 120–38.

Norcott, G. (2018a) 'Interview with Christopher Hope: Audiences are bored of Brexit themed comedy', 27 July, *Chopper's Brexit Podcast*.

Norcott, G. (2018b) 'Brexit voter stereotypes', Comedy Unleashed, 21 June, https://www.youtube.com/watch?v=imCGfN-GZHg (accessed 11 October 2019).

Odysseous, L. (2001) 'Laughing matters: peace, democracy and the challenge of the comic narrative', *Millennium* 30(3): 709–32.

O'Neill, B. (2017) 'Britain's comics can't stand Brexit – but the joke is on them', *The Spectator*, 6 April, https://blogs.spectator.co.uk/2017/04/britains-comics-cant-stand-brexit-joke/ (accessed 11 August 2019)

Orwell, G. (1945) 'Funny, but not vulgar', *Leader Magazine*, 28 July, http://orwell.ru/library/articles/funny/english/e_funny (accessed 14 August 2019); republished in *The Collected Essays, Journalism and Letters of George Orwell*, London Penguin, 1968, p 781.

Rorty, R. (1989) *Contingency, Irony, and Solidarity*. Cambridge: Cambridge University Press.

Rossdale, C. (2019) *Resisting Miltarism: Direct Action and the Politics of Subversion*. Edinburgh: Edinburgh University Press.

Sabur, R. (2017) 'Comedians claim anti-Brexit jokes are damaging their careers as audiences outside London walk out in offence', *The Telegraph*, 4 April, https://www.telegraph.co.uk/news/2017/04/04/comedians-tell-anti-brexit-jokes-damaging-careersas-audiences/ (accessed 11 October 2019).

Salter, M. (2011) 'No joking!', in V. Bajic and W. de Lint (eds) *Security and Everyday Life*. New York: Routledge, pp 31–48.

Saunders, R. (2009) *The Many Faces of Sacha Baron Cohen: Politics, Parody and the Battle Over Borat*. Lanham, MD: Lexington Books.

Sayle, A. (2007) 'Bernard Manning and the tragedy of comedy', *The Independent*, 20 June, http://www.independent.ie/entertainment/bernard-manning-and-the- tragedy-of-comedy-26438527.html (accessed 12 August 2020).

Sayle, A. (2013) 'Alexei Sayle: I'm still full of hate', *The Guardian*, 22 January, https://www.theguardian.com/stage/2013/jan/22/alexei-sayle-still-full-hate (accessed 4 September 2019).

Sayle, A. (2014) 'Interview with Richard Herring', *Richard Herring's Leicester Square Theatre Podcast*.

Sayle, A. (2016) *Thatcher Stole My Trousers*. London: Bloomsbury.

Schaffer, G. (2016) 'Fighting Thatcher with comedy: what to do when there is no alternative', *Journal of British Studies* 55(2): 374–97.

Scott, J.C. (1987) *Weapons of the Weak: Everyday Forms of Peasant Resistance*. New Haven, CT: Yale University Press.

Scott, J.C. (2012) *Two Cheers for Anarchism: Six Easy Pieces on Autonomy Dignity and Meaningful Work and Play*. Princeton, NJ: Princeton University Press.

Seabrooke, L. (2010) 'What do I get? The everyday politics of expectations and the subprime crisis', *New Political Economy* 15(1): 51–70.

Sillito, D. (2017) 'How many pro-Brexit comedians are there?', BBC website, 5 April, https://www.bbc.co.uk/news/entertainment-arts-39507659 (accessed 11 October 2019).

Solomon, T. and Steele, B (2017) 'Micro-moves in international theory', *European Journal of International Relations* 23(2): 267–91.

Southwell, T. (1998) *Getting Away with It: The Inside Story of Loaded*. London: Ebury Press.

Steele, B. (forthcoming) 'A catharsis of anxieties': insights from Goffman on the politics of humour', *Global Society*.

Sutton, A. (2019) 'Generalised comedy production', paper presented at workshop on 'Humour and Global Politics', University of Warwick, 7–8 May.

Sutton, A. (forthcoming) 'Generalised comedy production: British comedy production and stand-up', *Global Society*.

Tilley, L. and R. Shilliam (2018), 'Raced Markets: An Introduction', *New Political Economy*, 23(5): 534–543.

Van Zoonen, L.t and Wring, D. (2012) 'Trends in political television fiction in the UK: themes, characters and narratives', *Media, Culture & Society* 34(3): 263–74.

Vintaghen, S. and Johansson, A. (2013) ' "Everyday resistance": exploration of a concept and its theories', *Resistance Studies* 1: 1–46.

Wagg, S. (1992) 'You've never had it so silly: the politics of British satirical comedy from *Beyond the Fringe* to *Spitting Image*', in D. Strinati and S. Wagg (eds) *Come on Down? Popular Media Culture in Post-war Britain*. London: Routledge, pp 254–84.

Wagg, S. (1996) 'Everything else is propaganda: the politics of alternative comedy', in G.E.C. Paton, C. Powell and S. Wagg (eds) *The Social Faces of Humour: Practices and Issues*. Aldershot: Ashgate, pp 321–44.

Wagg, S. (2002) 'Comedy, politics and permissiveness: the "satire boom" and its inheritance', *Contemporary Politics* 8(4): 319–34.

Ward, S. (2001a) 'Introduction', in S. Ward (ed.) *British Culture and the End of Empire*. Manchester: Manchester University Press, pp 1–20.

Ward, S. (2001b) 'No nation could be broker': the satire boom and the demise of Britain's world role', in S. Ward (ed.) *British Culture and the End of Empire*. Manchester: Manchester University Press, pp 91–110.

Watson, M. (2007) 'Towards a Polanyian perspective on fair trade: market based relationships and the act of ethical consumption', *Global Society*, 20(4): 435–51.

Weaver, S. (2011) *The Rhetoric of Racist Humour: US, UK and Global Race Joking*. London: Routledge.

Weaver, S. (2019) 'Brexit irony, caricature, and neoliberalism', in J. Webber, (ed) *The Joke is On Us: Political Comedy in Late Neoliberal Times*, New York: Lexington Books, pp 65–86.

Webber, J. (2013) *The Cultural Set Up of Comedy: Affective Politics in the United States Post 9/11*. Chicago: Intellect.

Wilmut, R. (1980) *From Fringe to Flying Circus*. London: Eyre Methuen.

Wilson, J. (2017) 'Hiding in plain sight: how the "alt right" is weaponizing irony to spread fascism', *The Guardian*, 23 May, https://www.theguardian.com/technology/2017/may/23/alt-right-online-humor-as-a-weapon-facism (accessed 14 August 2019).

Žižek, S. (2008) *The Sublime Object of Ideology*. London: Verso.

Index